Cambridge
IGCSE®

English
as a first language
Third Edition

ENDORSED BY

Cambridge
International Examinations

Cambridge IGCSE®

English

as a first language

Third Edition

John Reynolds

HODDER
EDUCATION
AN HACHETTE UK COMPANY

®IGCSE is the registered trademark of Cambridge International Examinations.

Although every effort has been made to ensure that website addresses are correct at the time of going to press, Hodder Education cannot be held responsible for the content of any website mentioned in this book. It is sometimes possible to find a relocated web page by typing in the address of the home page for a website in the URL window of your browser.

Hachette UK's policy is to use papers that are natural, renewable and recyclable products and made from wood grown in sustainable forests. The logging and manufacturing processes are expected to conform to the environmental regulations of the country of origin.

Orders: please contact Bookpoint Ltd, 130 Milton Park, Abingdon, Oxon OX14 4SB. Telephone: (44) 01235 827720. Fax: (44) 01235 400454. Lines are open 9.00–5.00, Monday to Saturday, with a 24-hour message answering service. Visit our website at www.hoddereducation.com.

© Ian Barr and John Reynolds 2001, 2005, 2013

First published in 2001

by Hodder Education,

an Hachette UK Company,

338 Euston Road

London NW1 3BH

Second edition first published 2005, reprinted 2006 (twice), 2008, 2009, 2010, 2011

This third edition published 2013

Impression number	5	4	3	2		
Year	2018	2017	2016	2015	2014	2013

Cover photo © bloomua – Fotolia

Illustrations by Integra Software Services Pvt. Ltd., Pondicherry, India

Typeset in 11/13pt ITC Galliard and produced by Integra Software Services Pvt. Ltd., Pondicherry, India

Printed in Dubai

A catalogue record for this title is available from the British Library

ISBN 978 1444 19166 0

Contents

Introduction

Your course

When choosing your route through the course, there are some important decisions that you and/or your teacher have to make.

The first decision is to select the appropriate examination level: Core or **Extended**. Your teacher will be able to explain in detail what is involved at each level, but the key points are as follows.

At both levels there are two compulsory areas of work:

- Reading Passages (Paper 1 (Core) **or** Paper 2 (Extended)) and
- Directed Writing and Composition (Paper 3) **or** the Coursework Portfolio (Component 4).

There is also a Speaking and Listening unit which is compulsory for candidates working within the UK National Curriculum (Syllabus 0522), and optional and separately endorsed for candidates from the rest of the world.

- For the assessment of Speaking and Listening, you can take the Test (Component 5) **or** do your speaking/listening as Coursework (Component 6).

The next decision is to choose between the Directed Writing and Composition (Paper 3) and Coursework Portfolio (Component 4).

Finally, unless you are a candidate for Syllabus 0522, you and/or your teacher have to decide whether or not you will take the Speaking and Listening option, and if so, whether you will do it as coursework or as an oral test.

Reading Passages (Paper 1 (Core) or Paper 2 (Extended))

- In Paper 1, there will be **two** reading passages. Understanding of them will be tested by a series of short-answer comprehension questions, a directed writing exercise based on the first reading passage and a summary.
- In Paper 2, there will be **two** reading passages. Understanding of the first passage will be tested by a directed writing task (based on the passage) and a task requiring an appreciation of the techniques used by the writer. Understanding of the second passage will be tested by a summary question.

Directed Writing and Composition (Paper 3) or Coursework Portfolio (Component 4)

Both these options require you to write at some length.

- If you sit the Directed Writing and Composition paper, you will have to produce **one** piece of directed writing, based on a passage or passages printed on the question paper and then choose one from four composition titles (two descriptive and two narrative) to produce a piece of continuous writing of between 350–450 words.
- If you are doing coursework instead of the examination, you will have to submit **three** pieces of written work, each of between 500–800 words. (One piece of informative/analytical/argumentative writing; one piece of descriptive/narrative writing and one piece of analytical writing in response to a text or texts chosen by your Centre.)

Speaking and Listening Test (Component 5) or Coursework (Component 6)

Assessment of Speaking and Listening skills does not contribute directly to your grade in Cambridge IGCSE First Language English. Candidates doing Syllabus 0522 are required to undertake this aspect of the IGCSE syllabus, and the grade they achieve will be recorded separately on their certificate. Speaking and Listening is optional for candidates taking other IGCSE First Language syllabus variants but it is worth remembering the following story which we were once told by a teacher in Cyprus.

A student followed a course which was not IGCSE and which did not offer the possibility of a Speaking and Listening unit. The student achieved success, getting a grade B, and on the strength of that was given a job in a bank. To their horror, her employers found that, although she could write letters, she had real problems when speaking to customers, either in the bank or on the phone. Without effective speaking skills, she had difficulties in doing her job well.

You might decide that it is worth doing the Speaking and Listening unit. There are, after all, four areas of skill when using any language: reading, writing, speaking and listening. Make sure you acquire them all.

Structure of the book

In this book you will find the chapters follow the requirements of the course very closely.

Chapter 1 aims to improve and develop your **reading** skills, to help you work to your best abilities in the Reading Passages paper (Papers 1 and 2).

Chapter 2 covers reading comprehension and other skills needed for the Directed Writing and Composition paper (Paper 3).

Chapter 3 looks at the particular skills needed when writing a summary – a task which features in both Paper 1 and Paper 2.

Chapter 4 aims to improve and develop your **writing** skills, to help you work to your best abilities in the Directed Writing and Composition paper.

Chapter 5 helps you to practise the specific skills you will need for the writing aspects of the Extended Directed Writing and Composition paper.

Chapter 6 advises you on continuous writing and gives you the opportunity to develop the necessary skills for writing compositions in an examination (Paper 3).

Chapter 7 looks closely at the special skills required for writing tasks for the Coursework Portfolio (Component 4) and gives advice and examples on how to approach these.

Chapter 8 gives you some opportunities to practise for the Speaking and Listening Test (Component 5) or prepare for your Speaking and Listening Coursework (Component 6).

Author's note: In the examples of students' work throughout the book, the original spellings and punctuation have been retained. Many errors are identified but many are left unmarked, reflecting the principle that teachers reward merit in writing and do not seek only to highlight mistakes.

Teacher's comments: are written in red like this

Teacher's analysis: is printed in blue like this

Note: All of the questions and answers that appear in this book and on the accompanying CD have been written by the author.

Becoming a better reader

● Why do you read?

The written word is all around us. It is almost impossible to spend a day without reading something. Here are a few examples.

- If you catch a bus, you will probably read the destination board to make sure that it is the bus that you need.
- If you go to a fast-food restaurant, you need to read the menu before deciding which meal you are going to order.

- Whenever you use a computer, you need to read the different messages that appear on the screen.

● When you settle down to relax after a hard day's study, you might decide to watch television. How do you find out which programmes are on? Most probably you will look at a television guide. How do you know when the programme you intend to watch is about to start? Almost certainly because you will read the title as it flashes up on the screen in front of you.

● Of course, you may decide that the most enjoyable way to relax is not by watching television at all, but by reading. But what will you read? Will you choose your favourite sports magazine or will you return to the novel that you left by your bed last night?

● Passive and active reading

So, reading is something we spend our lives doing, often without being conscious of the fact that we are doing it. In fact, you might think that the printed word is so much a part of our lives that we take very little notice of it; it is just *there*. We take it for granted and, as a result, we frequently recognise familiar (and less familiar) words without really thinking about what they mean – we're reading **passively**, just accepting what we see. Most of the examples given earlier are of passive reading, but reading can be an **active** process, in which you really think about what you are seeing and try to get as much out of the text as you can. It is important that you develop the skill of **active reading**, in other words **reading for understanding**.

An English Language examination, such as Cambridge IGCSE First Language English, is unlike most other subjects in that there are very few facts and details which you need to revise in advance. However, it is still important to spend time developing the **skills** you need. For Cambridge IGCSE First Language English you need to be able to:

- demonstrate understanding of explicit meanings
- demonstrate understanding of implicit meanings and attitudes
- analyse, evaluate and develop facts, ideas and opinions
- demonstrate understanding of how writers achieve effects
- select for specific purposes.

If you improve your skills in active reading, this will help you in many other school subjects as well.

An English Language examination will test your reading of different types of materials. You might be presented with:

- a piece of non-fiction (possibly taken from a newspaper)
- an extract from a novel or short story
- a piece of personal writing such as an autobiography to give just three examples.

Remember that words alone are not the only way by which writers convey meaning: pictures, diagrams, sub-headings, changes of font and typeface are all means by which writers will try to influence your responses as a reader.

How do you develop the skill of active reading?

Throughout your course, it is a good idea to practise reading a wide range of different types of writing. So, as well as reading novels and magazines, spend some time reading:

- newspaper articles – in particular, feature articles in which the writer develops an argument
- any leaflets or pamphlets you can find.

Remember, work in other subjects, such as History or Sociology, also requires you to read non-fiction books which contain complicated and well-structured arguments. As a general rule, try to read as wide a range of non-fiction as you can.

When you are reading, make sure that you think carefully about what the words, sentences and paragraphs actually mean. It may help to:

- ask yourself questions as you go along, or
- imagine what you would ask someone else if they had read the article and you hadn't.

When you are working on comprehension passages in class, it is almost certain that your teacher will keep asking you questions, to help you gain a complete understanding of what you have read, and to ensure that your answers are as precise and specific as possible. So, when you are reading on your own, try to think about what questions your teacher would ask if he/she were there with you. This should help to ensure that you have thought about the main concerns of the passages and understood them to the best of your ability.

Once you have mastered this approach, you will find that you are reading with a much clearer and more focused understanding – this will allow you to maximise the use of your skills in any examination.

● Skimming and scanning – getting the gist

During an examination, you need to be able to read as much as you can and understand it as fully as you can, in a limited period of time. This is why developing your active reading skills is so important. You must read through the whole question paper carefully, but if you are skilled at reading actively, then you can save some time by employing the techniques known as **skimming** and **scanning**. **Skimming** means reading quickly through a passage in order to gain a clear, overall view of what it is about. **Scanning** is a refinement of this approach, as it means you are reading in order to extract specific details which are relevant to the questions that you are required to answer. Before we look a little more closely at how to apply these techniques, there is one other very important point to consider, and it is also one which is easy to overlook.

Identifying key words in a question

At the beginning of this section we mentioned the importance of reading through the whole question paper. This means, of course, not only reading through the passages but also reading through the *questions* on those passages. A clear understanding of exactly what the question requires will help you to focus on those parts of the passage in which the relevant points can be found.

When you are reading a question, you may find it useful to underline the **key words**. For example, look at this summary question based on the passage 'A Whale of a Time in Oz!' (pages 5–6).

> Read carefully the passage 'A Whale of a Time in Oz!' and then summarise what it tells us about the behaviour of Southern Right Whales and why they were considered to be so suitable for hunting.

From your skimming of this question, you will pick up that the passage is about Southern Right Whales. The key words to underline as part of your scanning process are the instruction *summarise* and then the specific details on which you are to focus: *behaviour* and *why they were so suitable for hunting*.

Skim, scan and select

Now we can look at how skimming and scanning work when reading the passage itself.

1 **Skim the text.** You will notice that there is a **title**, followed by a **smaller title** (**sub-heading**). There is also a **photograph** with a **caption**, and an **extracted quote** two-thirds of the way through the article. These all contain details which can be easily taken in when you first skim/scan the page. They give you a quick, overall view of the subject of the text and the writer's attitude towards the subject. It is important that you make use of clues of this sort when you set out to read the passage.
2 **Scan the text.** Pick out details relevant to the question which you now have firmly fixed in your mind.
3 **Select the points you intend to use.** By scanning, you weed out those details which are not relevant to your purpose.

For this question you are being asked to identify **facts** about the whales and about why they were hunted. It is important that you understand the distinction between facts and opinions. **Facts** are objective details which can be supported by evidence. **Opinions** are subjective views held by the writer and cannot, therefore, be proved as being either right or wrong. Sometimes you may need to separate facts from opinions to show that you can distinguish between them. Or you may simply have to identify one or the other. Look again at the question on this passage (page 4). It asks only for factual details. You should, therefore, include only those in your answer. Having a clear understanding of this difference will make it easier to eliminate irrelevant opinions from your summary.

With these guidelines in mind, we will now look at the passage.

A Whale of a Time in Oz!

In search of the Southern Right Whale 'down under'

Helen Highwater

A Southern Right Whale and calf

The first few paragraphs set the scene. Although you will be taking the details in as useful background information, you will also be aware that the Southern Right Whale does not receive a mention until the third paragraph. If you are reading actively, you will immediately notice this and be alert for further information which is going to follow.

Getting there wasn't easy. First there was a 500 kilometre flight from Adelaide on a tiny plane shaped like a toothpaste tube. Then once we'd landed we met up with Gary White, our expedition leader, and his jeep. 200 kilometres along the Eyre Highway we entered the treeless Nullarbor Plain, a semi-desert populated mainly by Aborigines.

Our destination was the head of the Great Australian Bight, where we were to spend two days watching whales. On the way Gary told us what we wanted to know:

'Sadly, over 25,000 whales had been killed before whaling ceased in 1930. By this time Southern Right Whales were virtually extinct. They were known as "Right" whales because they were right for hunting in small land-based boats. They came close inshore, floated when killed, and had thick blubber, which produced the valuable whale oil when it was boiled down. This meant that the poor whales were hunted down in vast numbers by money-making shipowners.' ▶▶

As you read through the third and fourth paragraphs, it is likely that you will be asking yourself questions such as 'What do these details tell us about the whales' behaviour?', 'What was it about their behaviour which made them so easy to hunt?', and so on.

As you move on through the passage, you will find that it alternates between giving facts about the whales' behaviour and details about the scenery, and the writer's personal response to seeing the whales as they frolic in the water. The details of the scenery and the writer's opinions may make the passage interesting but you should be skimming over them as they are not details specifically connected to the questions which you are asking yourself.

In general, the language in which the passage is written is not difficult to understand and can be read quite easily by an average student. The vocabulary, for the most part, does not consist of long and complicated words. However, in the last-but-one paragraph the writer uses some more complicated sentences.

'Right Whales feed on small creatures at or near the surface, gently swimming along with their mouths half open, allowing the sea water to flow in. The water is pushed back out with their tongues, leaving the food behind. Thankfully, they are now a protected species and numbers have risen to nearly 800.'

This was a dismal tale but it had a happy ending – the whales were now safe from murderous whale hunters.

Two hours before sunset we arrived at our destination. The crumbling limestone cliffs dropped sheer into the deep blue of the bay. It was August, the height of the whales' breeding season. Every three years the whales come from their home waters in the Antarctic to their Australian breeding grounds. Mature females weigh 80 tonnes. The females do not eat at all until they return to the Antarctic. By this time they will have lost 20 tonnes in weight.

As the sun began to set behind us we looked out, but saw . . . nothing. Then boom! Right in front of us the sea erupted as a huge whale burst from the surface, thrusting its body out of the water and smashing down with a noise like a cannon firing. Again and again it surged from the sea, a majestic and thrilling sight.

After a meal under the stars we talked some more. Gary told us that large numbers of female whales and their calves had been in the bay the previous week. The calves are six metres long at birth and they grow to three times that length.

'This was Nature at its finest, awesome and strangely moving.'

Our final day began early. We packed up our camp, walked to the cliff edge and were amazed! I counted 24 whales. Swimming parallel to the shore, very close in, was a long procession of mothers and their calves. They floated past on the surface. Some swam side by side, others lazily rolled over each other as they moved slowly along. They were enormous. As they expelled the air from their blow-holes, great spouts of misty waters shot upwards. This was Nature at its finest, awesome and strangely moving. We were silent watchers of a primeval, wonderful sight. How can people hunt such beautiful and truly amazing creatures?

All too soon we had to go. In October the whales would return home too, home to the Antarctic. We said little. We'd been stunned by the size of Australia, climbed Ayers Rock and followed the tourist trail. These would become distant memories, but our two days whale-watching would remain alive in our hearts for ever.

Here, both the sentence structures and the vocabulary are more complicated. It is a good idea to slow down your skim reading at this point and stop to consider exactly what the words mean. Do these sentences contain information relevant to the question? If they do, then you need to consider how best to put the information into your own words to show a reader that you have understood. (Lifting the sentences as they stand and transferring them directly into your answer will be a sure sign that you do **not** understand them!)

Even if your understanding of the vocabulary used in these sentences is not entirely secure, your awareness of what the question is actually requiring you to look for should convince you that these are references to the writer's feelings or opinions. They do not have a great deal to do with the whales themselves, apart from telling us how impressive they are, which is a point made elsewhere in the passage anyway. You can safely pass over them and continue to read the passage. It will not then take you long to finish, as the remaining sentences may be of general interest in helping us to understand the writer's feelings but are not relevant to the material for which you are searching.

As you can see from this example, **selection of details** in your reading is vitally important to working under examination conditions. You must have a clear idea of what you are looking for and then focus on finding it and ignoring irrelevant comment or detail (which teachers refer to as **distractors**). The more swiftly you can select the facts and opinions that you actually need to answer the questions, the more time you will have for expressing your understanding of them as clearly as you can. Writing your answer will be dealt with in more detail in Chapters 2 and 3.

The reading you will be required to do in an examination will not always consist of non-fiction, factual material. Sometimes it will involve an extract from a short story or novel, such as the passage about Leela's friend (pages 19–20).

Remember: concentration and alertness help to make you a good reader. The more you practise your reading skills, the better your examination performance is likely to be.

● Practise your active reading skills

Here are some examples of the different types of reading passages which you may be given in an examination. Practise reading through them and see how easily you can grasp their meaning. Remember to try to focus on what seem to be their main concerns as you read.

Exercise 1

The extract below is a straightforward piece of informative writing.

- Its intention is to explain something to you, and when you are reading it you are likely to be scanning it for useful facts and details.
- Unlike the passage about spotting whales in Australia, it does not contain any photographs or sub-headings which may help to convey the writer's meaning. You will, therefore, need to think carefully about the meaning as you read through it. Try to identify the main points of the writer's argument and separate them from the examples he gives to illustrate them.

Study tip

A useful tip when reading this type of writing is to assume that each new paragraph deals with an important new point. If you can identify what we call the **topic sentence** in each paragraph, you will have found a good 'hook' on which to hang your understanding. For example, in the third paragraph of this passage the opening sentence is clearly the topic sentence. It states the main point of the paragraph and then the following sentences develop this point. Spotting the topic sentences helps you to keep a tight control over your understanding of a writer's argument.

Man is, pre-eminently, the animal who communicates, but until little more than a hundred years ago his thoughts could travel abroad no more swiftly than the sailing ship or the running horse.

The great change began when lightning itself became a messenger for mankind. At first, the electric telegraph was regarded as a superfluous novelty, but within a single lifetime engineers had spun a cocoon of copper wires around the world. In 1886 was laid the first successful Atlantic cable. From that moment, Europe and America were only seconds, and no longer days, apart. However, even when the telephone was invented in 1876 it was not possible to *speak* across the Atlantic; the early submarine cables could carry only telegraph messages. They were too sluggish to respond to the hundredfold-more-rapid vibrations of the human voice. Although a transatlantic telephone service was opened in 1927, it depended entirely on radio, which meant that even at the best of times conversations were liable to fadings and cracklings, and to eerie, Outer Space whistles and wails.

▶▶

The first transatlantic telephone cable went into service in 1956. As a result of the vastly improved service, there was an immediate jump in the number of calls between Europe and America. More cables had to be laid – first across the Atlantic and later across the still wider expanses of the Pacific.

By the dawn of the Space Age, therefore, the problem of inter-continental telephone calls had been solved – but it had been solved so successfully that it had raised yet more problems. The cables could carry only a limited number of conversations, and it seemed unlikely that they could keep up with the rising demand. Moreover, just as the Victorian cables could not cope with the telephone, so the submarine cables of the 1950s were unable to deal with the latest miracle, television – and for very similar reasons. The electric signals involved in the transmission of TV pictures were a thousand times too complex to be handled by a cable. A new breakthrough was needed and the satellites provided it in the nick of time.

From *Voice Across the Sea*, by Arthur C. Clarke, Harper and Row, 1958

Exercise 2

The passage below is taken from a newspaper article. It contains some graphical and layout features which are typical of this type of writing. When you practise reading this article, focus on trying to get a clear picture of what actually happened to Tony Bullimore. In order to make the article more immediate and dramatic, the writer has not described the events in a strictly logical sequence.

'Thank God . . . it's a miracle'

The thud of a fist and Briton is saved from cruel seas

Report by Ian Burrell

The rescue

It was the thud of a fist on the hull of Tony Bullimore's overturned yacht that told him he was not going to die.

The British yachtsman had spent four days and four nights in an air-pocket inside his capsized yacht, praying that he would be saved. 'I started shouting, "I'm coming, I'm coming",' he said. 'It took a few seconds to get from one end of the boat to the other. Then I took a few deep breaths and I dived out.'

It was the culmination of one of the most dramatic sea rescues of all time. Mr Bullimore had been stranded more than 1,500 miles from the Australian coast and 900 miles from Antarctica. The key to Tony Bullimore's incredible feat of endurance was an ability to remain calm and methodical in his thinking despite the most appalling circumstances.

The ordeal

Trapped in darkness, with freezing waters lapping at his feet and buffeted by 60ft waves, he will have known only too well that he was more than 1,000 miles from the nearest land.

Faced with the danger of being dragged down with the boat, most people would have been tempted to try and jump clear.

Mr Bullimore's sense of calm, developed from years of solo yachting, taught him otherwise. He stayed with the yacht and quickly took stock of the few straws available for him to cling on to.

Yesterday he described the horrific conditions that he had endured.

'Two-thirds of the hull filled with water. There was a hole in the bottom of the hull, in fact really at the top, where one of the windows had come out. This caused water to be sucked in and out at a colossal rate, causing a kind of Niagara Falls, but upside down.

> *'This chap is not an ordinary person like you or me.'*

'I had to find myself a spot as high up as possible and put nets around it so that I could crawl in there and lash myself in to get out of the water and to get away from everything.'

Dr Howard Oakley, of the Institute of Naval Medicine, said keeping a clear head and a sense of order were vital. Once he had decided to stay with the yacht, Mr Bullimore's priorities were to activate the distress beacon transmitter and to ensure he was getting enough air. Perched in a makeshift hammock, Mr Bullimore was alone with his thoughts, with nothing visible to focus on. This is the kind of situation that makes people motion sick.

Yet the discomfort of sea-sickness could not break Mr Bullimore's remarkable spirit.

'This chap is not an ordinary person, like you or me,' said a clinical psychologist, Eileen Kennedy.

'The kind of person who takes part in a solo yacht race welcomes challenge and risk.'

The survivor

The yachtsman said that during the 'horrific, traumatic experience' he was 'hanging on in there and believing something would happen and just fighting.'

Through four days of darkness and solitude, he depended on 'sheer determination, a little water, a little chocolate' to sustain him.

> *'It was just determination, a little water, a little chocolate . . . hanging on in there.'*

But even Mr Bullimore was at his endurance limit.

'I only just made it. Because of weather conditions, I was deteriorating at a reasonable rate,' he said. 'When I knew that the rescue was actually going to happen, I felt ecstatic.'

Adapted from an article in the *Independent*, 1998

② Applying your reading skills

Examinations at all levels contain questions that test your ability to show an understanding of the passages printed for you to read in the question papers. Although different papers use different types of questions to do this, success in an examination depends very much on the care and concentration with which you read. It is a good idea to keep the following points in mind when you set about preparing to answer questions:

- You have plenty of time to read the passages carefully; don't rush into writing your answers until you have gained a clear understanding of what you have been asked to read.
- Remember that careful reading and a clear understanding of the **questions** is as important as reading the passages. This will help to ensure that you are in the best position to select the details that are relevant to the question you are answering.
- Read each passage through carefully from beginning to end in order to gain a general, overall understanding of it: it is important that you gain a sound **overview** of what it is about.
- Once you have achieved both an overview of the passage and a clear understanding of what the questions require, then look closely at the relevant sections of the passage on which the questions are based. It may help to underline or highlight key points in the text so that you can easily find them when writing your answers.
- The next step is to produce your written answers to the questions. Remember: it is important that what you write makes clear that you have understood exactly what the question requires. A reader can judge your understanding only by what you have written; don't leave out points which may seem obvious if they are relevant; if you don't include a point, you cannot be given credit for knowing it.
- Make sure that the details you include in your answers are relevant to the question.
- Write your answers clearly without irrelevant comments.
- Use your own words as far as possible to demonstrate your understanding. If you are asked to explain the meaning of a word such as 'exciting' remember that an answer which says 'something that makes you feel excited' will not be sufficient, as you need to use a word such as 'thrilling' to show your understanding.
- Remember: the more marks a question is worth, the more detailed your answer should be. You may have to refer to more than one part of the passage to provide a complete answer.

● Types of questions

Passages which test your comprehension skills will be factual, narrative, descriptive or argumentative writing. The types of questions are likely to vary, depending on the type of passage.

The more straightforward questions set for Core or Foundation Curriculum papers will probably follow the order of the original passage – that is, the answers to the earlier questions will be found in the first part of the passage, and so on. In particular, the earlier questions may require you to find factual details from the passage, but later, more demanding questions may ask you to **interpret** some of the points included in the passage to arrive at your answer. It is not expected that you provide a right or wrong answer to this type of question; what is important is that you give evidence that you have understood the details of the passage and can apply this to produce a consistent interpretation of the question. This is particularly important if you are asked to write in character for a directed writing response.

How to approach short-answer comprehension questions

In this section we are going to look at some techniques that are specific to short-answer comprehension questions, such as those that might be set in Core or Foundation Curriculum examination papers. The example of a question paper which follows is worth a total of 20 marks and consists of a number of short-answer questions and a longer question, which is sub-divided, testing your response to the writer's use of language.

> **Note:** The questions on the passage that follow are simply examples of the types of questions that *might* be set for an examination; it is important that you become familiar with responding to a range of questions of this type.

Short-answer questions are straightforward. They require brief, factual answers to show that you have understood a particular piece of information in the text. You should try to express your answers in your own words.

Some questions will be worth more than one mark. Remember: the more marks there are available for a question, the more detailed and focused your answer should be.

The way in which a question is worded will give you some indication of the approach you should take in your answer. For example:

- Questions which contain instructions such as 'Give two reasons' require straightforward retrieval of details from the passage. Remember that you should provide two distinct reasons and not just two aspects of the same reason!
- Questions which ask you to 'Explain' something such as the writer's opinions, require you not only to say what the opinions are, but also to make some comment about them in your own words.
- Questions which begin 'Why do you think' the writer uses certain words or expressions (for example), require you to interpret and explain the writer's intentions in choosing these words. There are no specific right or wrong answers to these questions – remember to justify your opinion.

The lost lagoon

Philip Smith

Yellow and black, it was hiding among the sun-bleached branches at the water's edge. Our boat nudged closer to the island. I lifted my camera and pulled the creature's beady eyes into focus. Then, in a quarter of a second, measured by the camera's rapid frame-burst, the anaconda snapped open its jaws, sprang forward, and hissed in my face. In the Esteros del Iberá, I learned, it's hard to avoid getting up close and personal with nature.

Our guide, Maximo, was smiling. There was no danger, he told me. Anacondas aren't poisonous – they squeeze their victims to death. I can't have looked convinced because he quickly edged the boat away from the bank, and soon we were threading our way through the streams and inlets that weave an unknowable pattern through the embalsados – hundreds of floating islands which bump and skitter across the surface of this vast lagoon system, in a kind of slow-motion game of dodgems.

The Esteros del Iberá is the least known of Argentina's natural wonders. Its 63 lagoons are spread across an area the size of Wales and mark the former course of the Paraná River. In these vast wetlands an improbably rich ecosystem thrives, but until recently it received only a passing mention in many guidebooks. Only now, with a flurry of low-rise, eco-friendly development, is the Esteros finally opening up to tourism.

To reach the Esteros from Buenos Aires we took an overnight coach to the dusty town of Mercedes. After a further hour's journey in a 4×4 truck down the dirt track otherwise known as 'provincial route 40' and as a red sun crawled over the horizon, we approached the makeshift bridge which serves as a gateway to the Laguna Iberá. Iberá means 'bright water' in Guarani, and as we rattled over the bridge, the surroundings fell away as if we were driving across a gleaming ocean.

The sweeping lawns of the Posada de la Laguna were dotted with a selection of multicoloured birds. One had a shock of bright red head feathers, as if it had been dunked headfirst in a pot of Day-Glo paint. The birds barely noticed us; it was hard not to trip over them as we rolled our luggage through the freshly cut grass. Later, at breakfast, I turned to see a pair of hummingbirds on the veranda. They would return every morning.

We were staying in the small town of Colonia Carlos Pellegrini, an ideal base for exploring the Esteros. The posada was built in 1997, and in recent years a number of other lodges that share its emphasis on conservation and tradition have opened nearby. But none has such a privileged position, right on the water.

Walking to the small jetty, it was difficult to see where the posada's four acres of gardens ended and the water began, so dense was the covering of aguape and irupé: water hyacinths and lilies. As Maximo readied the boat, he told us that these plants spread so quickly he has to clear a new path through the water each morning.

We pushed away from the jetty, thrilled by a glimpse of a basking yacaré. Soon, sightings of this South American alligator would prompt little more than a nod of recognition. It seemed that every few metres you could spot a leathery snout and pair of prehistoric yellow eyes poking through the water.

Due to their relatively small size, the yacaré are generally not considered to be fatally dangerous to humans.

The yacaré feast on the local fish. Fat and happy, they pose little threat to humans. And some say it's OK to swim, as long as you don't mind the odd nibble from the palometas, a type of piranha found in these parts. I decided that any swimming would be confined strictly to the hotel pool.

When the Esteros became a natural reserve in 1983, hunting was banned and indigenous Guaranis like Maximo retrained as guides. Each day we explored a secluded new site offering an uncanny array of river otters, bizarre spiders, carpinchos, yacarés, snakes, butterflies and howler monkeys. We would hear rumours of a beautiful rare deer that constantly seemed to elude us. And then there were the birds. Almost 400 species call these marshes home. Some are difficult to miss, such as the chaja, that resembles an ugly turkey and emits a gurgling scream. Others take a little searching out: kingfishers, heron, ibis and eagles.

The lagoon system is so vast we rarely saw another boat. The wildlife here works in shifts, so when the daytime gang clocks off, many rarer creatures show their faces. Back among the water lilies where we had spent our first afternoon, we continued our search for the elusive marsh deer. Here the islands had rearranged themselves so extravagantly that, for the first time, even Maximo looked a little confused. As dusk turned to night and the darkness became inky black, he flicked on a powerful torch.

There was a movement in the reeds. We edged closer. The torch picked out a pair of eyes. And then, finally, there it was. A marsh deer standing glorious in the landscape, the furry tufts of its ears lit up by the tungsten glow of the torch. It turned its gaze towards us for a moment and then, with a twitch of the nose, disappeared into the darkness. It had been worth the wait.

Adapted from the *Guardian*, 29 November 2008

---

1 From paragraphs 1 and 2, give two facts that the writer gives about the anaconda.   (2 marks)

This is a question requiring straightforward interpretation and you are told exactly where to find the answer so you won't need to include information from anywhere else. A correct answer would be something similar to: 'Anacondas have "beady eyes"; they are not poisonous; they squeeze their victims to death.' Note: saying that anacondas are snakes would not be correct as this fact is not mentioned in the first two paragraphs. As is often the case in a structured question paper, this first question is a 'settling in' question.

---

2 What made the lodge in Colonia Carlos Pellegrini, in which the writer stayed, different from other lodges in the region?   (1 mark)

Again, this is a straightforward question; the answer is that the lodge is the only one in the region that is on the water's edge.

> 3 By referring closely to paragraph 9, explain, using your own words, what the writer says about swimming in the Esteros. (2 marks)

This question requires simple interpretation, although you need to reword the original statement to demonstrate your understanding. A good answer would contain the following details:

- the writer is not fully convinced that the creatures living in the water would not do him any harm
- he would much prefer to swim in the safety of the lodge's swimming pool.

> 4 Using your own words, explain what you learn about the life of Maximo from paragraph 10. (2 marks)

Notice that this question is clearly focused on the *life* of Maximo and is, therefore, testing specifically your understanding of not just what he does, but also what the word 'indigenous' tells you about him. A good answer would contain the following points:

- he is a native/original inhabitant of the area
- after the Esteros became a natural reserve in the 1980s, he was trained as a guide for visitors.

> 5 Which word in paragraph 11 tells you that the marsh deer was difficult to find? (1 mark)

This is a straightforward question requiring you to identify the single word 'elusive'. It is important that you quote only the actual word and not the whole sentence which contains it (unless you make it clear by underlining which word you have chosen).

> 6 By referring to paragraphs 3 and 11 explain, using your own words:
>   a) what the Esteros del Iberá is and how it was formed (2 marks)
>   b) what feature of the Esteros caused Maximo to look confused while searching for the marsh deer. (1 mark)

Again, this is a straightforward question requiring you to explain some details from the passage in your own words. Remember, as there are 2 marks available for the first of the sub-questions, you should attempt to identify two distinct details about the Esteros and how it was formed. A good answer to both parts of the question would contain the following details:

- The Esteros consists of 63 lagoons./It covers a very large area of land.
- It was originally part of the Paraná River which has now changed its course but has left the lagoons behind.
- The islands in the Esteros are floating vegetation and are in continual movement which makes navigation difficult.

> 7 a) Explain, using your own words, what the writer means by the words in italics in three of the following phrases:
>
>   i) 'hundreds of floating islands which bump and *skitter* across the surface'
>
>   ii) 'One had a shock of bright red head feathers, as if it had been *dunked* headfirst in a pot of Day-Glo paint.'
>
>   iii) 'a secluded new site offering an uncanny array of river otters, *bizarre* spiders, carpinchos, yacarés, snakes, butterflies and howler monkeys'
>
>   iv) 'The wildlife here *works in shifts*, so when the daytime gang clocks off, many rarer creatures show their faces.'　　　　　　　　　　　　　　(1 mark each)
>
> b) Explain how the words and language used by the writer in each of the phrases you have chosen help to suggest the particular fascination of the Esteros region and the creatures that live there.　　　　　　　　　　　　　　(2 marks each)

This question requires some response to the language the writer uses. It is worth 9 marks in total; 1 mark would normally be awarded for an explanation of the meaning of each of the three words/phrases selected, and a further 2 marks for an explanation of how the writer's choice of words/imagery helps to convey the fascination of the region and the creatures that inhabit it. With questions of this type, it is important in your answers to distinguish between the first part which requires a straightforward *explanation* of the meaning of a word, and the second part which requires a comment on how the words used by the writer help to create a particular response in the mind of the reader. For example:

ai) The word *skitter* means to skim or glide across a surface (in this case, water).

bi) The choice of the verbs *bump* and *skitter*, with their associations with fairground rides, suggests the unpredictability and frequency with which the islands are changing shape and position.

aii) The word *dunked* means to dip something into a liquid (such as a biscuit into a cup of tea).

bii) The choice of the word *dunked* suggests something done without a great deal of care and effectively conveys the almost haphazard arrangement of the brightly coloured feathers in the bird's crest. The reference to *Day-Glo paint* also suggests a cartoon-like quality of the brightly coloured bird.

aiii) The word *bizarre* means unusual, freakish and incongruous.

biii) The choice of the words *uncanny* and *bizarre* suggests that the creatures living in the region are unlike anything found anywhere else on earth, and that they are highly unusual and unexpected. Also, these creatures are found in a *secluded* area which their appearance contrasts with and so emphasises their unusual appearance. The use of the word *array* suggests that they are deliberately putting themselves on show for the visitors.

aiv) The phrase *works in shifts* means that each member of the wildlife in the region has its own scheduled period when it performs in front of the visitors.

biv) The comparison of the wildlife to the workforce in a factory gives the creatures human characteristics. It suggests that their lives are organised into a carefully planned pattern of appearances so that the most persistent of visitors are rewarded with an entertaining variety show.

● Practise answering reading comprehension questions

Exercise 1

You will probably find the following extract easier to understand than some of the more informative writing you have already looked at. Be careful, therefore, that you do not fall into the trap of reading it passively. It is important that you continue to **concentrate on extracting the meaning** as fully as possible. With this type of writing you are not looking just to identify relevant facts but also, for example, to indicate an understanding of the motives and personalities of the characters described. Think about this as you answer the questions which follow the passage.

First read the extract. The writer describes the effect of severe weather conditions on her father's farm in Australia.

After the great rain of 1939, the rainfall declined noticeably in each successive year. In 1940, the slight fall was of no consequence because our major worry was that the accumulation of growth on the land would produce serious bushfires. These did occur on land quite close to us, but my father's foresight in getting cattle to eat down the high grass preserved Coorain from that danger.

In 1941, the only rain of the year was a damp cold rain with high wind which came during the lambing season in May and June and carried off many ewes and their newborn lambs. After that there were no significant rainfalls for five years. The unfolding of a drought of these dimensions has a slow and inexorable quality. The weather perpetually holds out hope. Storm clouds gather. Thunder rolls by. But nothing happens. Each year as the season for rain approaches, people begin to look hopefully up at the sky. It mocks them with a few showers, barely enough to lay the dust. That is all.

It takes a long time for a carefully managed grazing property to decline, but three years without rain will do it. Once the disaster begins, it unfolds swiftly. So it was with us.

My father and I would set out to work on horseback as usual, but instead of our customary cheerful and wide-ranging conversations he would be silent. As we looked at sheep, or tried to assess the pasture left in a particular paddock, he would swear softly, looking over the fence to a neighbour's property, already eaten out and beginning to blow sand.

Each time he said, 'If it doesn't rain, it will bury this feed in a few weeks.' It was true and I could think of nothing consoling to say.

His usual high spirits declined with the state of the land, until the terrible day when many of our own sheep were lost because of a sudden cold rain and wind when they had too little food in their stomachs. By 1942 it was apparent that the drought could be serious.

Shortly afterwards, the first terrible dust storm arrived boiling out of the central Australian desert. One sweltering late afternoon in March, I walked out to collect wood for the stove. Glancing towards the west, I saw a terrifying sight. A vast boiling cloud was mounting in the sky, black and sulphurous yellow at the heart, varying shades of ochre red at the edges. Where I stood, the air was utterly still, but the writhing cloud was approaching silently and with great speed. Suddenly I noticed that there were no birds to be seen or heard. All had taken shelter. I called my mother. We watched helplessly. Always one for action, she turned swiftly, went indoors and began to close windows. Outside I collected the buckets, rakes, shovels and other implements that could blow away or smash a window if hurled against one by the boiling wind. Within the hour, my father arrived home. He and my mother sat on the back step not in their usual restful contemplation, but silenced instead by dread.

A dust storm usually lasts days, blotting out the sun, launching banshee winds day and night. It is dangerous to stray far from shelter, because the sand and grit lodge in one's eyes, and a visibility often reduced to a few feet can make one completely disorientated. Animals which become exhausted and lie down are often sanded over and smothered. There is nothing anyone can do but stay inside, waiting for the calm after the storm. Inside, it is stifling. Every window must be closed against the dust, which seeps relentlessly through the slightest crack. Meals are gritty and sleep elusive. Rising in the morning, one sees a perfect outline of one's body, an after image of white where the dust has not collected on the sheets.

As the winds seared our land, they took away the dry herbage, piled it against the fences, and then slowly began to silt over the debris. It was three days before we could venture out, days of almost unendurable tension. The crashing of the boughs of trees against our roof and the sharp roar as a nearly empty rainwater tank blew off its stand and rolled away, triggered my father's recurring nightmares of France during World War 1, so that when he did fall into a fitful slumber it would be to awake screaming. It was usually I who woke him from his nightmares. I, the child in the family, would waken and attempt to soothe a frantic adult.

▶▶

When we emerged, there were several feet of sand piled up against the windbreak to my mother's garden; the contours of new sandhills were beginning to form in places where the dust eddied and collected. There was no question that there were also many more bare patches where the remains of dry grass and herbage had lifted and blown away.

It was always a miracle to me that animals could endure so much. As we checked the property, there were dead sheep in every paddock to be sure, but fewer than I'd feared. My spirits began to rise and I kept telling my father the damage was not too bad. 'That was only the first storm,' he said bleakly. He had seen it all before and knew what was to come.

From *The Road from Coorain: An Australian Memoir*, by Jill Ker Conway, Vintage, 1992

Note: The marks allocated to each question, for this and any subsequent exercises, are given as a guide only and should not be taken as a definitive representation of an actual examination mark scheme.

---

1   What do we learn about the rainfalls in this part of Australia in the years 1939, 1940 and 1941? (3 marks)

2   Which one word does the writer use in paragraph 6 to describe the results of the lack of rain? (1 mark)

3   Explain, using your own words, why the writer's father was worried about the lack of rain (paragraphs 5–6). (2 marks)

4   What two things led to the deaths of many sheep on 'the terrible day'? (2 marks)

5   Re-read paragraph 7 from 'Shortly afterwards . . .' to 'We watched helplessly.' and explain, using your own words, what were the main signs of the approaching dust storm. (4 marks)

6   Write a summary of the dangers and problems caused by a dust storm (paragraphs 7–9, from 'Always one for action . . .' to 'to awake screaming.'). (7 marks)

7   Re-read the end of paragraph 9 (from 'The crashing . . .' to 'a frantic adult.') and explain what you think the writer means by this section of the passage. (3 marks)

8   In the second to last line of the passage, why do you think the writer uses the word 'bleakly' to describe how her father spoke? (2 marks)

9   Re-read paragraphs 4–7. Give three words or phrases which describe the father's thoughts, and explain what each of them tells you about his state of mind during this period. (6 marks)

Exercise 2

Read carefully the passage 'Leela's Friend' and then answer the questions which follow.

LEELA'S FRIEND

The young boy Sidda was hanging about the gate at a moment when Mr Sivasanker was standing in the front veranda of his house, brooding over the servant problem.

'Sir, do you want a servant?' Sidda asked.

'Come in,' said Mr Sivasanker. As Sidda opened the gate and came in, Mr Sivasanker looked at him hard and said to himself, 'Doesn't seem to be a bad sort . . . At any rate, the fellow looks tidy.'

'Where were you before?' he asked.

Sidda said, 'In a bungalow there,' and indicated a vague somewhere, 'in the doctor's house.'

'What is his name?'

'I don't know, master,' Sidda said. 'He lives near the market.'

'Why did they send you away?'

'They left the town, master,' Sidda said, giving the stock reply.

Mr Sivasanker was unable to make up his mind. He called his wife. She looked at Sidda and said, 'He doesn't seem to me worse than the others we have had.' Leela, their five-year-old daughter, came out and gave a cry of joy. 'Oh, Father!' she said, 'I like him. Don't send him away. Let us keep him in our house.' And that decided it.

Sidda was given two meals a day and four rupees a month, in return for which he washed clothes, tended the garden, ran errands, chopped wood and looked after Leela.

'Sidda, come and play!' Leela would cry, and Sidda had to drop any work he might be doing and run to her, as she stood in front of the garden with a red ball in her hand. His company made her extremely happy. She flung the ball at him and he flung it back. And then she said, 'Now throw the ball into the sky.' Sidda clutched the ball, closed his eyes for a second and threw the ball up. When the ball came down again, he said, 'Now this has touched the moon. Come. You see here a little bit of the moon sticking.' Leela keenly examined the ball for traces of the moon and said, 'I don't see it.'

'You must be very quick about it,' said Sidda, 'because it all will evaporate and go back to the moon. Now hurry up . . .' He covered the ball tightly with his fingers and allowed her to peep through a little gap.

'Ah, yes,' said Leela. 'I see the moon, but is the moon very wet?'

'Certainly, it is,' Sidda said.

'What is in the sky, Sidda?'

'God,' he said.

'If we stand on the roof and stretch our arm, can we touch the sky?'

'Not if we stand on the roof here,' he said. 'But if you stand on a coconut tree you can touch the sky.'

'Have you done it?' asked Leela.

'Yes, many times,' said Sidda. 'Whenever there is a big moon, I climb a coconut tree and touch it.'

▶▶

'Does the moon know you?'

'Yes, very well. Now come with me. I will show you something nice.' They were standing near a rose plant. He said, pointing, 'You see the moon here, don't you?'

'Yes.'

'Now come with me,' he said, and took her back to the yard. He stopped near the well and pointed up. The moon was there, too. Leela clapped her hands and screamed in wonder, 'The moon is here! It was there! How has that happened?'

'I have asked it to follow us about.'

Leela ran in and told her mother, 'Sidda knows the moon.' At dusk he took Leela in and she held a class for him. She had a box filled with catalogues, illustrated books and stumps of pencils. It gave her great joy to play the teacher to Sidda. She made him squat on the floor with a pencil between his fingers and a catalogue in front of him. She had another pencil and commanded, 'Now write.' And he had to try and copy whatever she wrote in the pages of her catalogue. She knew two or three letters of the alphabet and could draw a kind of cat and crow. But none of these Sidda could copy, even remotely. She said, examining his effort, 'Is this how I have drawn the crow? Is this how I have drawn the *B*?' She pitied him and redoubled her efforts to teach him. But that good fellow, though an adept at controlling the moon, was utterly incapable of plying the pencil. Consequently, it looked as though Leela would keep him there, pinned to his seat, until his stiff, inflexible wrist cracked. He sought relief by saying, 'I think your mother is calling you in to dinner.' Leela would drop the pencil and run out of the room, and the school hour would end.

From *Malgudi Days*, by R.K. Narayan, Penguin, 1994

1 Which word in sentence 1 suggests that Mr Sivasanker is concerned about something?   (1 mark)
2 Describe, using your own words, Mr Sivasanker's first response to the boy, Sidda.   (2 marks)
3 Explain, using your own words, the phrase 'giving the stock reply'.   (2 marks)
4 What do you learn about Leela from the episode with Sidda and the ball?   (4 marks)
5 Give two details which show that Sidda is an imaginative boy, and explain why you have chosen them.   (4 marks)
6 Re-read the final paragraph and explain, using your own words, how Leela treats Sidda when she is 'teaching' him.   (4 marks)
7 From the same section of the passage, choose two words or expressions which show that Sidda was not good at his lessons, and explain why you have chosen them.   (4 marks)
8 In line 7 what do you think the writer means by using the expression 'indicated a vague somewhere'?   (2 marks)
9 Write a summary of all you have learned about the history and character of Sidda from this passage.   (7 marks)

Exercise 3

Read carefully the passage 'The new school' and then answer the questions which follow.

THE NEW SCHOOL

A young girl named Esther goes to a new school in Russia when her family are exiled from Poland, in 1941.

The morning I was to go to school for the first time, I woke up in a blackness as mysterious as the heart of a dark forest, the sounds nearby its strange beat. But the howl of a wolf way out in the country gave me my bearings.

I took up my little notebook, and a small stub of pencil, my only academic possessions. How long would they last? How small could I write?

I quickly got dressed, as warmly as I could, although deep winter had not yet arrived. I pulled a sweater over my thin little blouse, and struggled into my black leather shoes, which were not only pinching but which were beginning to crack from the wet and the mud, and endless drying in front of our little stove. On went my one and only coat. I was ready to go.

Mother had to be at the bakery early that day and so, clutching my notebook and pencil, I went to school alone. It never occurred to me that for a child to walk alone down a deserted Siberian road, so obviously a stranger, required some courage. I was too busy trying to rehearse the Russian alphabet I would need to know in my new school.

In room number five, a few children in caps and coats were seated at their desks watching the teacher write on the blackboard. She turned when I came in and looked at me so severely my heart sank.

'You must be Esther Rudomin. From Poland. Your Russian will be poor.' It was as if she was reading from a dossier that would determine some sort of punishment. 'It will be my task to see that you improve it. My name is Raisa Nikitovna. Go to the last desk of the third row and sit down.'

Without another word, she picked up a book, and called out a page number. Everyone had a book but me. The feeling must have been something like being the only soldier without a gun. I leaned towards the girl next to me and asked if I might share her book. She grudgingly agreed. She was a very pretty girl with short blonde hair, and eyes the special blue of northern countries. I asked her name, but she told me to be quiet; there was absolutely no talking allowed in class.

My first lesson in school in Siberia was memorable for being a chilly one. It was not only the Russian author's meaning that evaded me, lost as it was in a sea of strange letters formed in the Russian alphabet, but so did the book itself – literally. My classmate somehow managed to keep slipping it out of my field of vision, which forced me to strain, squirm, and nudge her to bring the book closer. Naturally, I had barely read the first paragraph when Raisa Nikitovna began to quiz the class. To my horror, one question was directed at me. As I began to answer in my halting Russian, all the children turned to stare at me.

▶▶

When the lesson was finished, Raisa Nikitovna introduced me to the class: 'This is Esther Rudomin, who comes from Poland. As you can tell, she does not know Russian well and she will have to work hard to catch up. She will share her books with Svetlana. Stand up, Svetlana.' Svetlana turned out to be the pretty little girl sitting next to me; the prospect of *sharing* with her was not heartening. The more attention I got in class, the more she sulked. I sensed that Svetlana wanted to be the queen bee and that I had become her natural enemy. This was confirmed when I asked if I might come to her house and study with her. The answer was a sharp 'No!' I would be allowed to go there to fetch books when she had quite finished with them, but otherwise I could jolly well trot home and study alone.

At the end of my first day at school, I went home and collapsed on the sofa. Out of the confusion of the day, three giants emerged to be slain: Svetlana, Raisa Nikitovna, and the Russian alphabet.

From *The Endless Steppe*, by Esther Hautzig, Puffin, 1993

1 Give two details, from paragraphs 2 and 3, which suggest that Esther's family were poor. (2 marks)
2 Why did Esther's mother not accompany her to school? (1 mark)
3 Explain, using your own words, what worried Esther most on her way to school. (3 marks)
4 Describe, using your own words, the way Esther was treated and what her feelings were when she first met her new teacher. (3 marks)
5 What were the problems Esther had when she tried to read the book? (3 marks)
6 Explain what is meant by the word 'halting' in the phrase 'my halting Russian'. (1 mark)
7 Re-read paragraph 9. Choose three words or phrases which Esther uses to describe Svetlana and explain what they tell us about Svetlana's character. (6 marks)
8 Re-read the last paragraph. Explain fully, using your own words, what Esther meant by her reference to the 'three giants'. (4 marks)
9 Write a summary of what happened to Esther during her first day at school and what her thoughts and feelings were at different times of the day. (7 marks)

Exercise 4

Read carefully the extract from *The First Men in the Moon* on pages 23–24, an early work of science fiction written by H.G.Wells and published in 1901. Then answer the questions which follow. The story tells of the adventures of the narrator, Bedford, and an eccentric scientist, Cavor, as they explore the surface of the moon having travelled there in a spherical space capsule, invented by Cavor. (Our knowledge of space travel and conditions on the moon has increased significantly since Wells wrote this book!)

SUNRISE ON THE MOON

As we saw it first it was the wildest and most desolate of scenes. We were in an enormous amphitheatre, a vast circular plain, the floor of the giant crater. Its cliff-like walls closed us in on every side. From the westward the light of the unseen sun fell upon them, reaching to the very foot of the cliff, and showed a disordered escarpment of drab and greyish rock, lined here and there with banks and crevices of snow. This was perhaps a dozen miles away, but at first no intervening atmosphere diminished in the slightest the minutely detailed brilliancy with which these things glared at us. They stood out clear and dazzling against a background of starry blackness that seemed to our earthly eyes rather a gloriously spangled velvet curtain than the spaciousness of the sky.

The eastward cliff was at first merely a starless selvedge to the starry dome. No rosy flush, no creeping pallor, announced the commencing day. Only the Corona, the Zodiacal light, a huge cone-shaped, luminous haze, pointing up towards the splendour of the morning star, warned us of the imminent nearness of the sun.

Whatever light was about us was reflected by the westward cliffs. It showed a huge undulating plain, cold and grey, a grey that deepened eastward into the absolute raven darkness of the cliff shadow. Innumerable rounded grey summits, ghostly hummocks, billows of snowy substance, stretching crest beyond crest into the remote obscurity, gave us our first inkling of the distance of the crater wall. These hummocks looked like snow. At the time I thought they were snow. But they were not – they were mounds and masses of frozen air.

So it was at first; and then, sudden, swift, and amazing, came the lunar day.

The sunlight had crept down the cliff, it touched the drifted masses at its base and came striding with seven-leagued boots towards us. The distant cliff seemed to shift and quiver, and at the touch of the dawn a reek of grey vapour poured upward from the crater floor, whirls and puffs and drifting wraiths of grey, thicker and broader and denser, until at last the whole westward plain was steaming like a wet handkerchief held before the fire, and the westward cliffs were no more than refracted glare beyond.

'It is air,' said Cavor. 'It must be air – or it would not rise like this – at the mere touch of a sun-beam. And at this pace …'

He peered upwards. 'Look!' he said.

'What?' I asked.

'In the sky. Already. On the blackness – a little touch of blue. See! The stars seem larger. And the little ones we saw in empty space – they are hidden!'

Swiftly, steadily, the day approached us. Grey summit after grey summit was overtaken by the blaze, and turned to a smoking white intensity. At last there was nothing to the west of us but a bank of surging fog, the tumultuous advance and ascent of cloudy haze. The distant cliff had receded farther and farther, had loomed and changed through the whirl, and foundered and vanished at last in its confusion.

Nearer came that steaming advance, nearer and nearer, coming as fast as the shadow of a cloud before the south-west wind. About us rose a thin anticipatory haze.

Cavor gripped my arm. 'What?' I said.

'Look! The sunrise! The sun!'

He turned me about and pointed to the brow of the eastward cliff, looming above the haze about us, scarce lighter than the darkness of the sky. But now its line was marked by strange reddish shapes, tongues of vermilion flame that writhed and danced. I saw, a crown of fire about the sun that is forever hidden from earthly eyes by our atmospheric veil.

And then – the sun!

Steadily, inevitably came a brilliant line, came a thin edge of intolerable effulgence that took a circular shape, became a bow, became a blazing sceptre, and hurled a shaft of heat at us as though it was a spear.

It seemed to stab my eyes! I cried aloud and turned about blinded, groping for my blanket beneath the bale.

And with that incandescence came a sound, the first sound that had reached us from without since we left the earth, a hissing and rustling, the stormy trailing of the aerial garment of the advancing day. And with the coming of the sound and the light the sphere lurched, and blinded and dazzled we staggered helplessly against each other. It lurched again, and the hissing grew louder. I shut my eyes; I was making clumsy efforts to cover my head with my blanket, and this second lurch sent me helplessly off my feet. I fell against the bale, and opening my eyes had a momentary glimpse of the air just outside our glass. It was running – it was boiling – like snow into which a white-hot rod is thrust. What had been solid air had suddenly at the touch of the sun become a paste, a mud, a slushy liquefaction, that hissed and bubbled into gas.

There came a still more violent whirl of the sphere and we had clutched one another. In another moment we were spun about again. Round we went and over, and then I was on all fours. The lunar dawn had hold of us. It meant to show us little men what the moon could do with us.

From *The First Men in the Moon*, H.G. Wells

1 In paragraph 1 where are the explorers and their space craft? (1 mark)
2 Explain, using your own words, the meaning of the following words and phrases in italics as used in the passage:
   a) 'a *disordered escarpment* of drab and greyish rocks' (2 marks)
   b) 'The eastward cliff was at first *merely a starless selvedge* to the starry dome.' (2 marks)
   c) 'a thin edge of *intolerable effulgence*' (2 marks)
3 By referring to paragraph 3, explain, using your own words, why the explorers were able to see the scenery around them. (2 marks)
4 Explain fully, using your own words, the first effects of the appearance of the sun as described by the writer in paragraph 5. (4 marks)
5 Explain, using your own words, why the 'crown of fire' around the sun is not visible from Earth. (2 marks)
6 What effect does the writer achieve by the four-word paragraph, 'And then – the sun!'? (2 marks)
7 Explain, using your own words, the effect on the narrator of the appearance of the sun. (2 marks)
8 Re-read paragraphs 10–18 and then write a summary of everything that Cavor and the narrator saw as the sun rose. (7 marks)
9 Explain fully, using your own words, what happens to the explorers in the last two paragraphs of the extract. (3 marks)

● More complex comprehension questions/ How writers achieve effects

Some examination questions, especially those set for Extended or Higher Curriculum papers, will require more developed and longer responses, and may take different forms in order to test your reading skills. For example, you may be asked to produce a piece of continuous writing in which you show your understanding of a reading passage by using details from it with a different purpose from that of the original writer and addressing a different audience. Another type of longer question might ask you to write a detailed analysis of the writer's use of language and how it sets out to achieve a particular response from readers.

Understanding how writers achieve effects

All good writers are aware of their audience and choose their words carefully in order to persuade their readers to share their viewpoint. To do this, they will pay particular attention to the tone of voice they use. The **tone** or **register** of a piece of writing is produced not just by the choice of vocabulary, but also by the length and types of sentences used, the choice of similes and metaphors as well as the use of other literary devices such as **irony**, **rhetorical questions**, **alliteration** and so on. When you are analysing the way a writer uses language it is important that first you decide on the **purpose** of the piece of writing and the **audience** for whom it is intended. You should always keep these points in mind and refer to them when analysing a writer's use of language.

Emotive language

Words have different suggested meanings depending upon the context in which they are used; professional writers are very much aware of these associations and will use them to influence the way their readers respond to what is written. For example, think about the difference between these two sentences:

'On arrival at her uncle's house, she was given a cordial welcome.'
'On arrival at her uncle's house, she was given a hearty welcome.'

Both sentences give the same basic information to the reader, but the choice of adjectives ('cordial' and 'hearty') gives the reader different impressions of the warmth of the welcome the girl received. 'Cordial' suggests something much more formal than 'hearty', although the root meaning of both words is exactly the same. ('Cordial' derives from the Latin word for heart.) A sensitive writer, however, is aware of the different suggestions of the two words (much formal language in English derives from Latin vocabulary) and will choose 'hearty' to describe a friendly reception and 'cordial' to describe a more formal greeting.

Now look at this example: a newspaper article written exactly one year after the very powerful Hurricane Katrina smashed into the city of New Orleans in the USA. At that time, many streets were still looking like a war zone and bodies were still being found in the wreckage.

Read carefully the article 'Hell and high water' and then answer the questions which follow.

Hell and high water

Report by Paul Harris

Katrina's winds died a year ago, but they left deep scars. You see them in wrecked streets. You see them in destroyed forests. You see them in tiny white mobile homes that now dot the Deep South. You see them most, perhaps, in people's fearful expressions when a hard rain begins to fall from an angry summer sky.

Dr Becky Turner sees them in the play of children. Her big blue bus pulls up outside schools on the Gulf Coast of Mississippi and pupils walk in to use toys and paints. It sounds like fun. But what Turner and her colleagues see each day, drawn in crayon, is far from harmless.

When Dr Turner uses play to tease out the children's storm stories in order to help them talk about the horrors of their experiences, the horrors certainly do come. Many of the children of Hurricane Katrina lost relatives. Some saw them die. All of them are still living with the hurricane. And it is about to get worse. Turner and her staff are preparing for a flood of new cases as the anniversary approaches. 'It will be like a retraumatisation,' Turner says in a weary voice. 'The storm just goes on and on in their lives.'

So it does. Katrina hit on 29 August 2005 and, a year later, life on the coastline of Louisiana, Mississippi and Alabama is still a nightmare. Rebuilding scarcely seems to have begun. Gaunt ruins stretch for miles through a disaster area the size of Britain. All over America, from Houston to New York, hundreds of thousands of evacuees have been torn from their homes. Many expect never to return.

Bodies are still being found – this month a victim's skeleton was unearthed in New Orleans – yet Katrina is now an ignored tragedy. The hurricane slammed one of the poorest areas of the country. It had no respect for colour, creed or wealth, but its victims tended to be the most poor. After a year, the storm's victims are still living in limbo as the rest of the country has moved on. They are the forgotten ones.

Bienville Drive in the city of Waveland was a beautiful place to live. It was a winding road of large houses, populated mainly by retired people who came to Mississippi's Gulf Coast to relax in the warm weather by the sea. Jack Hyman, 72, was one of them. A gregarious ex-policeman who seems to know everyone in town, he and his wife, Fay, came here to settle. 'It was one of the best places in the world,' he says. 'Nothing much ever happened here.'

But it was in Waveland, 12 months ago, that Katrina made landfall. The storm had rolled up from the south, feeding on the warm waters of the Gulf, sucking up their energy into its screaming 240 kph winds. It smashed ashore, spawning tornadoes and bringing a tidal surge that poured inland.

There is little left of Waveland now. On Bienville Drive the houses have been reduced to pulp. It is as if the storm hit a month ago, not a year. Shops lie in ruins. The town's local government is run from a series of mobile homes. Many people survive on food handouts. Yet Jack Hyman is determined to stay. He and Fay live in a trailer supplied by Fema (the Federal Emergency Management Agency) in what used to be their front yard. 'It was like Katrina was a big bowling ball, and it just bowled down all these houses,' he says, a trace of awe in his voice.

That is why Becky Turner's travelling bus clinic, a project of the Children's Health Fund charity, is so important. In a region where adults have suffered so much, someone has to think of the children. Tonette Lagrone is an art therapist on the bus. She tells the story of a young girl who came aboard almost mute. The girl drew a picture of a blue box, floating on water. Gradually she opened up to Tonette. The girl's family had fled their home as the waters rose, eventually clambering into a blue dumpster bin. It was full of stinking, rotting rubbish. The family cowered inside it as the bin was washed away. By a miracle, they were rescued. Now the art therapy is working a second miracle. 'She's speaking again,' Lagrone says with pride.

Adapted from the *Observer*,
27 August 2006

1 Imagine that you are working as a volunteer with Dr Becky Turner's travelling bus clinic. Write a letter to your older sister who is living at home, encouraging her to join you in your work.
In your letter:
● give your impressions of New Orleans
● describe the suffering of the people you have met
● describe the worthwhile work you are involved in.
Base your letter on what you have read in the passage. Be careful to use your own words.
2 Re-read the passage and then, referring closely to the words and phrases used by the writer, explain how he conveys to his readers:
a) the after-effects of Hurricane Katrina on the city of New Orleans
b) the feelings of the city's inhabitants and of those such as Becky Turner who are trying to help them.
Remember to use quotations from the passage in your answer.

Answer techniques
Question 1

- It is important to remember that questions of this type test both reading and writing skills and that very often the marks allotted to the reading element are greater than those allotted to writing.
- When approaching a task such as this, you should ensure that you have a clear understanding of the precise details on which you should focus in the original passage. If the question contains bullet points indicating key topics (as on page 27), then it is a good idea to use the bullet points in structuring your response. It is likely that one of the bullet points may require you to make inferences based on implications contained in the passage – this bullet is likely to be a key discriminator and requires a thoughtful and developed response. Remember that your treatment of this must be based on ideas contained in the passage; made-up details with no basis in the original passage will not be considered evidence of understanding and will not score highly for the reading mark (although they may still be assessed independently under the writing criteria).
- Questions such as the one on page 27 require you to adopt a *persona* (in this case, that of a volunteer on the travelling bus clinic) and provide you with a genre for writing (a friendly letter) and an audience to whom your writing should be addressed (the volunteer's older sister).
- Remember: this is a letter to a close relative so you will be expected to adopt an informal tone and use appropriate salutation and valediction. ('Dear Miss …' and 'Yours faithfully' would be considered inappropriate, as their tone is more suitable to a letter written to someone with whom you have a more distant relationship.) However, you should also keep in mind that you need to show your ability to write accurately and clearly in English, so your letter should not be so full of colloquial expressions that technical accuracy is forgotten.
- It is also highly unlikely that you will be required to put an address at the top of your letter but will simply be instructed to begin your letter with 'Dear Sister …' or something similar.

Question 2

- Questions of this sort are intended to test your appreciation of the ways in which writers use language to produce a particular response from their readers. They require you to explore the suggestions and associations produced in a reader's mind by the writer's choice of vocabulary and imagery. For example, the opening paragraph contains words such as *scars, wrecked, destroyed, hard rain, angry summer sky*. The first three of these convey the seriousness and long-lasting effects of the damage caused by the hurricane (for example, both *wrecked* and *destroyed* suggest damage which cannot be easily repaired). The final two phrases suggest that this damage was caused by a malicious action of the sky which is using its extreme weapons such as hard rain (a term also associated with nuclear bombings) to vent its rage on the city. The word *summer* reinforces the unnaturalness of the event, as summer is usually seen as a time when the weather is benevolent.

● It is important to remember that this type of question tests your ability to explain how a writer uses language to manipulate the reader's response; although the passage may contain metaphors, similes and other figures of speech, the question is not asking you simply to identify them but instead to explain their effects. Consequently, a comment such as 'the phrase *angry summer sky* is a metaphor used to personify the sky and draws the reader into the article' will not score highly unless you continue to say *how* the metaphor helps to bring the sky clearly into the reader's mind and *why* it succeeds in engaging the reader with the passage.

Exercise

Read carefully the passage below in which the writer describes the after-effects of the Chernobyl nuclear disaster on the surrounding area, and then answer the questions which follow.

We head north and west from Kiev, making for the town of Narodichi. It's 60 km due west of Chernobyl, two of whose reactors, our guide reminds us, are still operational. The Ukrainian Parliament has voted unanimously to close them down. The Soviet government has refused. The Ukrainians claim 8000 died as a result of the accident. The official Soviet figure is 32.

We are passing through woodlands of pine and oak scrub interspersed with harvested fields and cherry and almond orchards. An army convoy of 40 trucks passes, heading south. After a while the woodland gives way to a wide and fertile agricultural plain. The first indication that this abundance is tainted comes as quite a shock. It's a sign, set in brambles and long grass, which reads, 'Warning: It is forbidden for cattle to graze, and for anybody to gather mushrooms, strawberries and medicinal herbs'.

We stop here and put on our yellow badges, which register radiation levels, and which will be sent back to England for analysis after our three-hour visit. Armed with these and a radiation detector, we enter Narodichi where people have lived with radiation for over five years. It's a neat, proud little town with a chestnut-lined main street and a silver-painted Lenin in front of the party headquarters. In a year's time there will be no one here.

In the municipal gardens the grass is uncut but a fountain still plays. There are several memorials. One is a scorched tree with a cross on it – local people think that the forest protected them from the worst of the blast. Beside the tree are three large boulders, one of which commemorates four villages and 548 people evacuated in 1986, another 15 villages and 3264 people evacuated in 1990. Twenty-two more villages and a further 11,000 people will be going in 1991. An inscription reads: 'In memory of the villages and human destinies of the Narodichi region burnt down by radiation.'

One of the most polluted areas is the children's playground, with 13 to 17 times normal radiation levels. The red metal chairs hang down from the roundabout and blue steel boats swing gently in the breeze, but no one is allowed to play here anymore.

Ivan, the local schoolmaster, is short and podgy and his face is an unhealthy grey. There were 10,000 children in the region, he tells me, now there are 3000. Two of his pupils pass by on bicycles and he grabs them and introduces us. The boys, just back from a Pioneer camp in Poland, look bored, and reply in monosyllables, which Ivan translates thus: 'The children send fraternal greetings to children throughout the United Kingdom.' He smiles proudly and a little desperately. I ask if the children's work has been affected by their proximity to Chernobyl. He sighs and nods.

'There is not a single healthy child here.'

▶▶

29

As we drive out of Narodichi, Ivan talks proudly of the history of his town, interspersing this with casually chilling present-day observations.

'This is the bridge over the Oush River. It is an area of the highest pollution.'

We come to the village of Nozdrishche, which was evacuated last year. There are no ruins, there is no devastation or destruction. Wooden cottages with painted window-frames stand in their orderly rows. Flowers are in bloom and grasshoppers dart around in lush overgrown gardens. It is a hot, soft, gentle summer's day. Yet scientists who have visited the area say it could be 700 years before this place comes back to life. It is hard to know what to believe, for whatever curse lies over these villages is the more frightening for being invisible. It is how one has heard the countryside would be after a nuclear war – benign, smiling, deadly.

A year's exposure to the weather has not yet dissipated a faint smell of disinfectant in a small, deserted maternity hospital. A poster on the wall depicts the American space shuttle spinning round the earth, with the single word 'Nyet!' beneath. There is a book on breastfeeding, its leaves nibbled by mice, an examination chair, medical records still in files, and a portrait of Lenin which has fallen out of its frame and lies in a corner beneath a scattering of glass slides and syringes. Conscious of the limited time we have been advised to spend here we move on through the village. I catch sight of two figures down a lane to one side of the main street. One is a very old lady, whose name is Heema, and the other her nephew. Heema is 90 years old and has refused to be moved from the village. She says she has been moved five times since the disaster and now she is too old and ill. Her one wish is to die in the house in which she was born, but that is now cordoned off with barbed wire, so she will remain here with her daughter. They are the only inhabitants of Nozdrishche.

Further along the road, at the village of Novoye Sharno, the radiation detector bleeps for the first time.

'Pay attention, please,' says Ivan, 'the radiation is very high here.'

This is one of the villages evacuated in 1986, immediately after the explosion and fire, and the village shop is now almost submerged in the undergrowth. Inside it is a mess of broken shelves, abandoned goods, smashed bottles.

'There was a panic here,' our guide explains, unnecessarily.

We drive back through Narodichi, where, as in Novoye Sharno and Nozdrishche and over 40 villages in this region alone, the grass will soon grow around doors that will never be opened again, and anyone who comes here will be informed of the dangers and the risks which those who lived here were not told about until it was too late.

From *Pole to Pole* by Michael Palin, BBC Consumer Publishing (Books), 1995

1 Imagine that you are Ivan, the schoolteacher referred to in the passage. You are visiting schools in other countries, including yours, to raise awareness of the problems suffered by people in the Chernobyl area. Write the words of the talk you would give to the senior students in your school. In your talk:
- describe the area in which you live(d) before and after the disaster
- describe the suffering and problems of the people who live(d) there
- suggest ways in which people in other countries can help those living in the Chernobyl area.
Base your report on what you have read in the passage. Be careful to use your own words.

2 Re-read the passage and then, referring closely to the words and phrases used by the writer, explain how he conveys to his readers:
a) the appearance of the area as a result of the nuclear disaster
b) the effects of the disaster on the lives and appearances of the people who live in the area.
Remember to use quotations from the passage in your answer.

Reading and summarising

Writing summaries is one of the main tasks that you will be required to do in an examination. Although it involves writing, it is your **reading** skills that will really determine your success in a summary question. It is also important that you keep a clear head when attempting the task.

Summaries come in different forms. You may have to:

- read one lengthy passage and summarise only the points contained in one or two paragraphs of it
- read one lengthy passage and summarise points related to a particular aspect or aspects of it which occur throughout the passage
- read two lengthy passages and summarise all the points relating to a particular aspect or aspects of them.

No matter what form the question takes, the basic principles of summary writing remain the same. What is important is that you show **evidence** that you:

- have **understood** what you have read
- can **select the relevant information**
- can express the information **using your own words** and **in a shorter form** than in the original.

Remember that you will never be asked to summarise a passage unless it is possible to do so by using fewer words than were in the original!

● Some practical guidelines

Whatever level of examination you take, your summary writing can be improved if you keep the following points clearly in your mind. Summary writing needs good planning and cannot be rushed. Most examination questions will give a clear indication of the number of words that you should aim to write; for example, 'You should write between 200–250 words.' although sometimes this might be expressed as something like 'about one side of the answer booklet'. As you can see, the writing itself will not take very long; the most important part of the process is **deciding what to include** and **what should not be included** – that's why your active reading skills are essential.

It is important to organise your time efficiently when answering a summary task and, as part of your preparation for an examination, you should look closely at past papers and decide how long you have available to answer the question. Remember that this time allowance includes reading the original passage(s), making notes of the relevant points and planning your answer. It is important that you spend most of the time available on these aspects of answering the question: if you have a clear understanding of what you are going to write for your final version, the actual writing of it will not take very long at all.

Once you have this basic approach clearly in mind, you can begin the task with confidence. Don't panic: remember, all the information you need to include will be in the original passage(s), so all you have to do is identify the really important points.

The following guidelines apply particularly to writing the type of summary based on aspects of a single, lengthy passage.

Note: Note-making is particularly important. Some examinations require you to write a list of main points which will be credited with marks before your final version of the summary.

Step 1: read the question carefully

This is very important, as it is unlikely that you will be required to summarise the whole of the original passage(s). The wording of the question will direct you towards the points you should include. For example, the whole passage may be about everyday life in Japan, but you may be asked to summarise only what it tells you about going to school in that country. You must, therefore, keep the wording of the question clearly in mind when reading the passage(s).

Step 2: read right through the passage(s) once

This will allow you to gain a good, overall understanding of what the material is about.

Step 3: identify the information that is relevant

Refresh your memory of what the question asks you to do and then read through the passage(s) again very carefully. At this stage you should underline or highlight on the question paper all the information that is relevant to the question. You must be ruthless. Ignore anything that is not relevant, no matter how interesting you may find it. It may help if you give your summary a title.

Study tips

1 Some points in the original passage may be harder to find than others – this may be because they are **implied** by the writer, rather than being explicitly stated. Your final summary will be more successful if you are able to identify and include these implied points.
2 You can safely **ignore**: illustrations, quotations, long descriptions and strings of adjectives.

Step 4: make notes in your own words

Now is the time to put pen to paper. You should make rough notes of the points you have identified, **using your own words** as far as possible. Remember, the use of your own words is important as this is a way of showing that you have understood the passage(s). Try to:

- **paraphrase (rephrase) parts of the text to which you refer**
- use synonyms – words with the same meaning – instead of the exact words from the text.

This will make it very clear that you understand what you have read.

Study tip

Check that you have made **each point only once**: it's an easy mistake to include three examples of the same point. The writer of the original passage is allowed to repeat ideas; you don't have the space to do so.

Step 5: count the main points

Once you have noted all the main points, count how many you have identified. If you have identified 20 points and you are aiming to write a summary of about 200 words, then, as a rough guide, try to write about ten words for each point.

> ## Study tip
>
> One of the main mistakes in summary writing is to use up too many words writing the early points, so the summary becomes top-heavy and unbalanced. Remember that all points should be given equal weighting.

Step 6: write the summary

Once you have written rough notes in your own words, you should write them up as a piece of continuous prose, trying to keep your expression as concise as possible. If your notes are sufficiently detailed, this may only be a fine-tuning job.

> ## Study tip
>
> An important word of warning – **do not include:**
>
> - personal opinions
> - extra information or explanations
> - your own comments or opinions on the points made in the original text(s)
> - quotations from the original passage(s).
>
> The readers of your summary do not want to know your personal opinions about the topic; instead, they want to know how well you have understood the original writer's viewpoint.

Step 7: final check

Once you have written your summary, read it through to check that it makes sense. You may not have to count the number of words you wrote. If, for example, you know that you usually write about eight words per line, then a quick count up of the number of lines you have filled will give some indication of how many words you have written in total.

> ## Study tip
>
> Summary tasks, unlike formal précis exercises, do not usually require you to write a specific number of words. Although a precise word limit is unlikely to be specified on a question paper, it is important that you try to express your understanding concisely within about one side of A4 paper. It is a good idea to focus your mind on this requirement when writing your answer. It is unlikely that a very long answer will gain the highest marks available for a question because you will not have shown your ability to select the key points and to stick to them. If you write considerably less than the suggested length, it is most probable that you will penalise yourself (and reduce your score) because it is almost certain you will have left out some of the important points.

● Style matters

In many summary questions, in addition to marks being awarded for the selection of the correct points, such as those listed on page 36, further marks may be available for written expression. It is, therefore, important that you take care with the quality of your writing as well as the content, as these marks could have a significant influence on your overall grade. Guidance as to what is good summary style is contained in the bullet points on page 35. Note that the copying of chunks of material directly from the passage will not score highly – this is because copying the text does not prove that you have understood it. It is important that what you write shows that you have understood the text and can interpret what you have read.

The following points should be followed very carefully; they contain some important advice.

- Concision of expression is something which typifies the very best summaries. This can be achieved by making sure that you focus clearly on only the points stated in the wording of the question.
- One way of doing this is to make sure that you don't include any irrelevant comments; a generalised introductory paragraph is not necessary and simply uses up unnecessary words.
- Lifting (or quoting) whole phrases or sentences from the original does not give a clear indication that you have understood the text.
- A summary should be written using an objective, impersonal register; there is no need to comment or to write in the first person – even if that is the way in which the original has been written.

Example of a summary question

The following example is suitable for students taking Core or Foundation Curriculum examinations to use for practice.

> The pilot of my balloon is a Swede called Lars and his co-pilot is his English wife Kali. They have flown all over the world but are almost as excited about today's flight as we are. The air will be both clear and cool. Visibility should be near-perfect.
>
> We're up in the sky about the same time as the sun, and for a while it is uncomfortably cold. The ride, though, is magnificent. The strange and unique landscape all begins to make sense as we rise above it. The eastern horizon is broken by the 12,848-foot peak of Erciyes Dagi, its summit partly ripped away by the eruption that helped shape everything we can see. Long, flat tables of rock mark the height of the plateau created by the vast lake of lava, most of it now cracked, fissured and fashioned into the bluffs, cones and tall pillars that cover the ground like sentinels of some petrified army.
>
> With the hard, bright sun at a low angle and a fresh-fallen blanket of snow on the ground, it's not only the rocks that stand out. We can see the fine detail of fields and orchards and vineyards. Though the volcanic rock makes for fertile soil, the climate has changed over the last few years and, according to Kali, the combination of warmer winters and late frosts has ruined harvests. Vines and apricot trees have been worst affected and certainly the apricot orchards look especially vulnerable under the snow. Many farmers are turning to tourism instead, or leaving the area altogether.
>
> Lars seems less interested in what's happening on the ground than what's happening in the air. He reads the air currents with obsessive delight, alert to all the subtle shifts and patterns, such as the emptying of the cold air from the valleys as the land warms up. He takes us up to 8,000 feet. From here the detail is less distinct. The rock forests of Cappadocia have given way to a wider view. From the Taurus Mountains in the south and to the rising Anatolian plateau to the east.
>
> From http://palinstravels.co.uk/book-4253

> Write a summary of what the passage tells you about what the writer saw from his balloon flight and his thoughts and feelings about the experience.
> You must use continuous writing (not note form) and use your own words as far as possible.
> Your summary should include all the points in your notes and must be 100–150 words.
> Up to 5 marks are available for the quality of your writing.

Model response

The passage has been annotated showing where the relevant points occur. The key points have been underlined.

What the writer saw

1 The <u>mountain</u>/peak of Erciyes Dagi
2 (Long,) flat tables of rock
3 Bluffs, cones and tall pillars
4 Bright <u>sun</u>
5 (Blanket of) snow
6 Fields and orchards
7 Less distinct details/wider view when higher up
8 Taurus Mountains/Anatolian Plateau

The writer's thoughts and feelings about the experience

1 He was excited.
2 He was initially feeling cold.
3 He found the ride magnificent.
4 He began to understand the <u>landscape</u>.
5 He thought that the apricot orchards were <u>under threat</u> from the <u>change in climate</u>.

Remember: you should focus on only including points that are directly relevant to the subject of the summary and pay close attention to the wording of the task. The question asks for a summary of what the writer saw from his flight and not what he saw during it. For this reason, it is not necessary to include Lars and his wife in your answer. Similarly, much of the third paragraph is not relevant as it is background information about the effects of climate change and not what the writer saw and thought during the flight (apart from his reference to the apricot orchards).

You will notice that in the list of points above (which is similar to those that would appear in an examination mark scheme) some words have been underlined. This indicates that the words are essential for the point to be credited. Other words are placed within brackets, indicating that these details are *not* necessarily required.

The points listed above can be turned into two paragraphs (one for what the writer saw and the other for his thoughts and feelings) which develop them into clear sentences.

At first, the writer saw the mountain, Erciyes Dagi, towering above the flat tables of rock and the bluffs, cones and pillars that rose from them. He saw the bright sun which allowed him a clear view of fields and orchards covered by a blanket of fresh snow. From 8000 feet the writer's view of the ground became less distinct but he could see a far greater distance, from the Taurus Mountains to the Anatolian Plateau.

The writer was very excited about his flight, especially as visibility conditions were perfect. At sunrise when they took off, he felt very cold at first but this did not prevent him from appreciating the magnificent ride. Seeing the landscape from the air made it easier for him to understand its formation, and the overview of the apricot orchard led to his appreciating how much farming in the area was threatened by climate change.

● Practise writing a summary

Having looked at the example and the model summary, you should now be able to write your own version using the points on page 36.

The following exercises are similar to those that might appear in Cambridge IGCSE First Language English examination papers for either Core or Extended Curriculums; use all or a selection of them as appropriate to practise your skills.

Exercise 1

Read carefully the report 'Nightmare Neighbours' and then answer these two summary questions. They are similar style questions to those which Core Curriculum students might encounter.

> 1 Summarise the problems caused by neighbours mentioned in the passage.
> 2 Summarise the advice given about how to deal with these problems.

Nightmare Neighbours

A clash with a neighbour can make life hell. And if things turn sour between you and your neighbour, you may not be able to get away from the problem – unless you move house.

For this report, we take the disputes which people have most often with neighbours and explain how to deal with each of them.

Noise next door can drive you mad. It could come from a barking dog or from non-stop, all-night parties. If you can't bear it any longer, contact the Environmental Health Department of your local council. You'll need to prove that the noise stops you from enjoying your property or that it is making you ill. You will need proof, so keep a diary.

Many house and car alarms seem to go off for no reason at any time of the day or night. If this is a problem, you can phone either the police or your local Environmental Health Officer. There is a new law which allows them to turn off a car alarm, and to enter premises to disconnect an alarm which keeps going off.

If your neighbours have the builders in, you may have to put up with drills and cement mixers. There is bound to be some disturbance; but if you cannot bear the noise, or it is taking place at night, then you can take them to court to make them stop work. This is called taking out an injunction.

If your neighbour's dog has bitten you, or frightens you, you will want to take action. Contact the local dog warden or the police. A court can order that a dog is muzzled and kept on a lead. If a dog continually enters and fouls your garden, the easiest thing to do is to put up a fence!

The parking place right outside your house is not part of your property. You have no legal right to park there. However, you have a legal right to enter your driveway or garage. Some local councils now operate parking schemes for residents. If your neighbours are always parking so you can't get out, contact the Highways Department of your local council. It is in charge of traffic management and control.

Call the police if you think your neighbour's parking habits are illegal.

If your neighbour fences off some of your land or starts growing plants in what you think is your garden then you have a problem. Arguments over land ownership are hard to solve. They can be sorted out in court but this could cost you a lot of money. You have to decide just how much time and money you are prepared to spend.

Some disputes are about party walls. These are walls built right on the boundary between homes. You and your neighbour are both responsible for these. You have to carry out repairs to your side of the wall. You cannot force your neighbour to repair his side.

If your neighbour's hedge or tree is hanging over your property, you can prune it back to the boundary but no further. You are not allowed to take fruit from a neighbour's tree just because the branches hang over your fence.

Many complaints are about neighbours' building extensions. People who wish to build extensions must have planning permission. The council must put up a notice at the site or write to all those who may be affected. You have 21 days to object to the proposal. Put your objection in writing and try to get other people to do so, too.

We hope that the information above will be useful. Good luck!

Adapted from *Which?* magazine

Exercise 2

Read carefully the following article and then summarise:

- what you learn about ancient Pompeii
- the work of archaeologists after the remains of the city were discovered
- the display in the National Museum of Singapore.

Pompeii exhibition opens at the National Museum of Singapore

The National Museum of Singapore transports visitors back 2000 years in time to experience life and death in the ancient Roman Empire. A new exhibition, Pompeii: Life in a Roman Village 79 CE reveals daily life in a city steeped in legend and mystery.

Pompeii and its neighbouring cities were buried – and frozen in time – after the fateful eruption of Mt. Vesuvius on August 24, 79 CE. After being forgotten for nearly 1700 years, the city was accidentally rediscovered by well-digging shepherds in 1748. Since then, its excavation has yielded extraordinary artifacts — from beds, lanterns, hairpins to an exquisitely preserved 15-foot-long garden fresco from the House of the Gold Bracelet—and provided a comprehensive portrait of the life of a city at the height of the Roman Empire.

Amazingly, archaeologists have also been able to piece together the final moments of the people of Pompeii. By pouring plaster into cavities in the volcanic ash left by the victims' bodies, archaeologists were able to create moulds of the final moments of life in this once-thriving seaport. The exhibition features more than 250 artifacts uncovered from beneath 30 feet of volcanic material in this once-cosmopolitan city. The exhibition brings these priceless artifacts, along with body casts of eight of the victims of Vesuvius' fury, to Singapore.

Many of the artifacts have never been on public display before 2007, including a stunning large-scale garden fresco, gold coins, jewellery, marble and bronze statuary, and other dazzling examples of ancient Rome's artistry and craftsmanship.

The exhibition takes visitors through an average day in Pompeii; visitors walk a Pompeian street complete with storefronts and ambient sound, see samples of food items carbonized by the eruption, explore a home and garden setting from Pompeii, and see how the people of Pompeii expressed their spirituality.

The showpieces of the exhibition are the body casts, made from the cavities left in the ash after the bodies of those buried decomposed. These figures are caught in their last moments, shielding their faces, clinging to each other. Even a dog impression was preserved.

Many objects buried beneath Pompeii were well-preserved for nearly 2000 years.

From *Archaeology News Network*, Art Daily, 18 October 2010

Exercise 3

Read carefully the following article and then summarise what it tells you about:

- plans for a channel tunnel before 1984
- the building and design of the present Channel Tunnel.

The Channel Tunnel

By Jennifer Rosenberg

The Channel Tunnel, often called the Chunnel, is a railway tunnel that lies underneath the water of the English Channel and connects the island of Great Britain with mainland France. The Channel Tunnel, completed in 1994, is considered one of the most amazing engineering feats of the 20th century.

For centuries, crossing the English Channel via boat or ferry had been considered a miserable task. The often inclement weather and choppy water could make even the most seasoned traveller seasick. It is perhaps not surprising then that as early as 1802 plans were being made for an alternate route across the English Channel.

This first plan, made by French engineer Albert Mathieu Favier, called for a tunnel to be dug under the water of the English Channel. This tunnel was to be large enough for horse-drawn carriages to travel through. Although Favier was able to get the backing of French leader Napoleon Bonaparte, the British rejected Favier's plan. (The British feared, perhaps correctly, that Napoleon wanted to build the tunnel in order to invade England.)

Over the next two centuries, others created plans to connect Great Britain with France. Despite progress made on a number of these plans, including actual drilling, they all eventually fell through. Sometimes the reason was political discord, other times is was financial problems. Still other times it was Britain's fear of invasion. All of these factors had to be solved before the Channel Tunnel could be built.

In 1984, the French and British agreed that a link across the English Channel would be mutually beneficial. However, both governments realized that although the project would create much needed jobs, neither country's government could fund such a massive project. Thus, they decided to hold a contest.

This contest invited companies to submit their plans to create a link across the English Channel. As part of the contest's requirements, the submitting company was to provide a plan to raise the needed funds to build the project, have the ability to operate the proposed Channel link once the project was completed, and the proposed link must be able to endure for at least 120 years.

Ten proposals were submitted, including various tunnels and bridges. Some of the proposals were so outlandish in design that they were easily dismissed; others would be so expensive that they were unlikely to ever be completed. The successful proposal planned for a tunnel made up of two, parallel railway tunnels that would be dug under the English Channel. Between these two railway tunnels would run a third, smaller tunnel that would be used for maintenance, including drainage pipes, communication cables, etc.

Some trains that would run through the Chunnel would carry passengers only. Other trains, known as 'shuttles', would be able to hold cars and trucks. This would enable personal vehicles to go through the Channel Tunnel without having individual drivers face such a long, underground drive. Also, large train terminals had to be built at Folkestone in Great Britain and Coquelles in France.

On December 10, 1993, the first test run was completed through the entire Channel Tunnel. After additional fine tuning, the Channel Tunnel officially opened on May 6, 1994.

Adapted from *About.com Guide*

Exercise 4

Read carefully the following article and then summarise what it tells you about:

- the state of women's football in the UK in 2012
- why women's football does not have the same public profile as the men's game
- how and why the Women's Super League (WSL) is using social media.

Women footballers bring new life to the beautiful game and score with Twitter

Tracy McVeigh

After years of feeling underrated and overlooked by mainstream football pundits and press, women's football is coming into its own this season thanks to social media.

New research shows that the women's version of the game is now the third biggest team sport in the UK in terms of participation, behind only men's football and cricket.

Its previous lack of recognition is being overcome by fans turning to social networking to follow the sport. The second ever season of the Football Association's Women's Super League (WSL) kicks off on Sunday, and eight of England's top female footballers, one from each of the top clubs, will take the unprecedented step of wearing their success on their sleeve by displaying their Twitter account names on their kit.

The new semi-professional league, the top tier of women's football, was launched by the FA last year as a platform to drive forward the women's game and the association claims that it will be spending £3m on promotion in the first three years of the league.

Since the WSL launched, attendances have increased by more than 600%, viewing figures of live broadcast matches, at 450,000, are on a par with those of the men's Scottish Premier League, and the social media channels now attract more than 80,000 followers. It has transformed the player–fan relationship by making it a fully interactive league. Research commissioned for the FA by Sport England Active People ahead of the 2012 season shows that the low profile of women's football is what is driving fans to Twitter and Facebook for news. Fans are up to seven times as interactive as those of the men's game.

The Fifa women's world cup was the most tweeted-about event in the world in July 2011 with 7,196 tweets per second at its peak. It remains seventh in the list of the most tweets per second, above the Uefa Champions League in 11th position.

But the findings show that while there are 12 times as many news articles with mentions of women's football per month, relative to the number of people who attend matches, men's football receives three times as many headlines, relative to the number of fans who attend.

'It is understandable in a way,' said England international and Arsenal Ladies midfielder Steph Houghton. 'It's difficult because the men's game is so big and attracts so much money and sponsorship and so it's always going to take priority.'

'But with digital media we can really forge ahead. We don't need to struggle to get a few lines in a newspaper, we can do it for ourselves; fans can interact with players and find out about fixtures and get really involved on match days – even if they are not at the game themselves.'

Houghton, 23, has been selected as the FA WSL digital ambassador for Arsenal Ladies this season. Each club in the league will pick one player who will wear their Twitter address.

'Twitter and Facebook have helped us massively, it's just transformed things over the past year,' Houghton said. 'It's really progressing the game. Our attendance figures have increased a lot. We're doing a lot of work in schools getting girls to play football, breaking down any taboos there might be, and we're seeing them get interested, and bring their families along where they have such a good match day experience that they're coming back.'

'I think that what's happening is that girls are enjoying playing. It's a lot more acceptable and now we have a Women's Super League with hugely dedicated female role models – really committed players who people can see are dedicated and training as hard if not harder than any male players – that's all progressing the sport. And with social media there's no holding women's football back.'

From the *Observer*, 7 April 2012

● More complex summary questions

The following example is typical of the type of summary question that you might find in an Extended or Higher Curriculum examination paper. It is based on a passage that is more demanding in content and linguistic expression than those that we have looked at so far. However, the technique required to write a summary of the passage is, in effect, very similar to that used to respond to the previous passages in this chapter. Read the passage and the question carefully and note down what you consider to be the main relevant points. Then read the analysis of the task that follows.

Dieting vs. Exercise for Weight Loss (1)

By Gretchen Reynolds

Two groundbreaking new studies address the irksome question of why so many of us who work out remain so heavy, a concern that carries special resonance at the moment, as lean Olympians slip through the air and water, inspiring countless viewers to want to become similarly sleek. (2)

And in a just world, frequent physical activity should make us slim. But repeated studies have shown that many people who begin an exercise programme lose little or no weight. Some gain.

To better understand why, anthropologists leading one of the new studies began with a research trip to Tanzania. There, they recruited volunteers from the Hadza tribe, whose members still live by hunting and gathering.

The researchers gathered data for 11 days, then calculated the participants' typical daily physical activity, energy expenditure and resting metabolic rates. They then compared those numbers with the same measures for an average male and female Westerner.

▶▶

It's long been believed that a hunter-gatherer lifestyle involves considerable physical activity and therefore burns many calories, far more than are incinerated by your average American office worker each day. And it was true, the scientists determined, that the Hadza people in general moved more than many Americans do, with the men walking about seven miles a day and the women about three. (3)

But it was not true that they were burning far more calories. In fact, the scientists calculated, the Hadza's average metabolic rate, or the number of calories that they were burning over the course of a day, was about the same as the average metabolic rate for Westerners. (4)

The implication, the scientists concluded, is that 'active, "traditional" lifestyles may not protect against obesity if diets change to promote increased caloric consumption.' That is, even active people will pack on pounds if they eat like most of us in the West. (5)

The underlying and rather disheartening message of that finding (6), of course, is that physical activity by itself is not going to make and keep you thin.

The overarching conclusion of that study, which was published last week in the journal PLoS One, is not really new or surprising, says Dr Timothy Church, who holds the John S. McIlhenny Endowed Chair in Health Wisdom at the Pennington Biomedical Research Center in Louisiana and who has long studied exercise and weight control. (7) 'It's been known for some time that, calorie for calorie, it's easier to lose weight by dieting than by exercise,' he says.

People stick with low-calorie diets more readily than they continue with exercise to drop pounds.

'There's an expectation that if you exercise, your metabolism won't drop as you lose weight or will even speed up,' says Diana Thomas, a professor of mathematics at Montclair State University in New Jersey.

But she says close mathematical scrutiny of past studies of exercise and weight loss shows that that happy prospect is, sad to say, unfounded. The problem for those of us hoping to use exercise to slough off fat is that most current calculations about exercise and weight loss assume that metabolism remains unchanged or is speeded up by exercise. (8)

So Dr Thomas has helpfully begun to recalibrate weight loss formulas, taking into account the drop in metabolism. Using her new formulas, she's working with a group of volunteers, providing them with improved predictions about how much weight they can expect to lose from exercise.

The predictions are proving accurate, she says, and although her forecast is for less weight loss than that under the old formula, the volunteers are pleased. 'It's better to meet lower expectations,' she says, 'than to be disappointed that you're not losing what you supposedly should.' She is perhaps her own best advertisement. In the past few years, she's shed 70 pounds and, using her formulas for how many calories she's actually burning each day thanks to a daily walk, has regained none of it. (9)

From The *New York Times*, 1 August 2012

Read carefully the passage and make notes of the main points. Then write a summary of what the passage tells you about:

- the research conducted with the Hadza tribe in Tanzania
- the findings of the studies carried out by Dr Church and Dr Thomas.

You should write between 200–250 words.

Model response

The purpose of this section is to help guide you through the process of writing a summary of this passage. Firstly, we will look at the thought processes of a student approaching the task and relate these to the highlighted sections. Next we will make numbered notes of the main points to be included. Finally, we will produce an example of a final summarised version of the points required by the question.

Thought processes

Sections of the passage highlighted in yellow are commented on below.

1 The title of the passage is a useful way of finding an overview; however, does it match the requirements of the question? In this case it does, so it's useful to keep the point in mind to help give a clear focus when writing the final version.
2 This is an interesting point as it relates the passage to the world of the reader but is not relevant to the topic of the summary, so it can be ignored.
3 This paragraph expands on the point made in the previous paragraph – it tends to make the same point again, but should the comparison with the lifestyle of American workers be included? It would help to link the two parts of the summary, so it should be included.
4 But this needs to be added to the point above.
5 This is an expansion of the key point made in the previous sentence but it does help to clarify it, so it would be useful to include it.
6 This is a subjective comment and not relevant to the summary topic.
7 The summary is about the *findings* of Dr Church's research – although his qualifications and position are impressive, it's not necessary to include them in a summary. 'Dr Church, an expert in exercise and weight control', would be more than enough.
8 There's certainly a relevant point being made in these two paragraphs but in rather a long-winded way, so it needs to be made more specific in a summary.
9 There's definitely a concluding point made here but, in the final summary, it's best to generalise it and remove the personal reference to Dr Thomas.

Sections of the passage highlighted in pink contain key points for the summary.

Notes

1   Research is being carried out into why regular exercise does not result in participants losing weight.
2   Researchers studied the Hadza tribe from Tanzania who are hunter-gatherers.
3   They studied their daily physical activity, how much energy they used and how this affected their metabolism (the chemical processes that take place in our bodies).
4   It was found that although the Hadza people were much more physically active than the average American, they did not necessarily burn more calories per day than people in America with different lifestyles.
5   This contradicts the expected findings; the conclusion to be drawn is that physical activity alone will not keep people thin, especially if people follow typical Western eating habits.
6   Dr Church states that this is not surprising; previous research has shown that it's easier to lose weight through a calorie-controlled diet than through exercise — and this appeals to people more.
7   The belief underlying many studies of weight loss is that exercise speeds up metabolism but Dr Thomas's findings do not support this. In fact, they indicate that metabolism may drop during exercise.
8   Consequently, she is revising the formulas associated with weight loss through exercise.
9   She is encouraging the volunteers with whom she is working to have lower expectations of the weight they can expect to lose.
10 Her predictions about weight loss are proving to be accurate, and the volunteers are satisfied with this and not disappointed that they are not losing more.
11 The evidence is that by following Dr Thomas's formulas relating to exercise and weight loss, people will lose weight and not put it back on again.

Final summary

It appears that regular exercise does not result in people losing weight. Researchers studied the hunter-gatherer Hadza tribe from Tanzania, in particular their daily physical activity, how much energy they used and how this affected the chemical processes that take place in their bodies (their metabolism). It was found that although they were much more physically active than the average American, they did not necessarily burn more calories per day than people in America with different lifestyles. The conclusion to be drawn is that physical activity alone will not keep people thin, especially if people follow typical Western eating habits.

According to Dr Church this is not surprising; previous research has shown that it's easier to lose weight through a calorie-controlled diet than through exercise — and this appeals to people more. Dr Thomas's findings do not support the belief that exercise speeds up metabolism and, in fact, indicate that metabolism may drop during exercise. Consequently, she is revising the formulas associated with weight loss through exercise. She is encouraging volunteers with whom she is working to have lower expectations of the weight they can expect to lose. Her predictions about weight loss are proving to be accurate, and the volunteers are satisfied with this and not disappointed that they are not losing more. The evidence is that by following Dr Thomas's formulas relating to exercise and weight loss, people will lose weight and not put it back on again. *(239 words)*

Exercise

Read carefully the article 'Genetically Modified Foods' and then summarise:

- what GM foods are and how they were developed
- the reasons given as to why they could be advantageous
- the concerns that some people in the UK have about GM foods.

Remember to make a list of key points and to use your own words as far as possible. You should write between 200–250 words.

Genetically Modified Foods

There has been much concern recently about GM foods, some of which are being tested and some of which are already used as ingredients in the food we eat. GM stands for 'genetically-modified', and describes the process by which scientists are able to pinpoint the individual gene which produces a desired outcome, extract it, copy it and insert it into another organism.

To some extent, humans have been involved in genetic modification for centuries. For example, larger cattle which gave more milk were bred to produce even larger offspring. Seeds from cereals and other crops that were hardier and grew better were selected for planting the following year to produce better yields. With genetically modified organisms however, the modifications involved are often of a kind that could not possibly occur naturally. For example, adding cow growth hormone to the embryo of a broiler chicken to produce a larger, faster growing chicken, or adding genes from a virus to a plant to allow it to become resistant to the virus.

There are many reasons why GM foods could be advantageous. For example, a crop could be made to grow quicker, with increased protein and vitamin levels, or with less fat. An often-used argument in favour of GM crops is that drought-resistant crops could help to alleviate famine in developing countries, where low rainfall often leads to food shortages. Techniques have also been developed to make fresh produce last longer, so that it can ripen on the plant and be transported more easily with less wastage.

The first GM food products – a tomato purée and a vegetarian cheese – appeared in British supermarkets in 1996. The purée was made from tomatoes which were designed to stay firmer for longer, leading to less waste in harvesting. The tomatoes also held less water, meaning that less water was required to grow them and less energy was used removing water from them to turn them into purée. This in turn made the purée cheaper for the consumer.

The first GM soya was planted in the US in the same year, and up to 60% of all products on supermarket shelves could now contain some GM soya. Monsanto, a major GM manufacturer, has developed a strain of GM soya which is resistant to Roundup, its own brand of herbicide. This allows weeds to be controlled even after the soya has started to grow, saving an estimated 33% on the amount of herbicide used. Roundup Ready® soya amounted to 15% of the 1997 US soya crop.

GM foods have been largely accepted by the Americans, with nearly 70% of them saying that they would buy GM foods even if they were simply engineered to stay fresh for longer. Even more would purchase foods modified to resist insect pests, resulting in less use of pesticides.

In the UK, people are being far more cautious, possibly with good reason. Lessons learned during the BSE crisis are still very much in people's minds. Can we trust what we are eating, and what could be the long-term effects?

▶▶

The UK has potentially more to lose by the introduction of GM crops. In America, farming takes place on an industrial scale, with millions of acres used exclusively for growing crops. Intensive use of pesticides has virtually wiped out wild animals and plants in the huge crop fields of the US. The Americans can afford to do this, as they also have many huge wilderness conservation areas often the size of several English counties, which are havens for all their native wildlife. In the UK however, farms are an integral part of the countryside. The use of herbicide – or insect-resistant crops – could potentially have severe effects on biodiversity, by virtually wiping out wild flowers and consequently the insects that feed on them, and further up the food chain, the predators that eat the insects.

Some crops are being developed to improve soil quality, by removing heavy metals from the soil, for example, so that they can be harvested and destroyed. An excellent idea, but what about the animals that eat the contaminated plants? Others are being developed for salt resistance, so that they can be grown in previously unusable areas. But what if their seeds were to be carried to a saltmarsh? Would they be a threat to wild species that have lived there naturally for years?

So far, there is no evidence of GM food being harmful to humans, but the rules governing their testing are less strict than with medicines, and after BSE, we know that 'no scientific evidence of harm' is not the same as 'safe to eat'.

Adapted from *Young People's Trust for the Environment*

● Further summary practice

In general, summary questions in examinations such as Cambridge IGCSE First Language English are usually based on factual, non-fiction passages. They require you to write a straightforward summary of the main details contained in the passage that are relevant to the specific requirements of the question that has been set. However, sometimes the passages used for summary are based on types of writing other than that which is intended to convey information. The following exercises are based on a range of types of writing.

- **Passage 1** is taken from a speech given by an American educator, in which he is putting forward a deliberately controversial view about education in the present day.
- **Passage 2** is an extract from Charles Dickens's *Bleak House* describing (and satirising the behaviour of) the eccentric Mrs Jellyby.
- **Passage 3** is a more conventional informative passage about the early history of advertising.
- **Passage 4** gives two different accounts of a visit to the Dutch theme park, Efteling, providing you with the opportunity to write a summary based on *two* passages.

The exercises relating to these passages allow you to approach summary writing in different ways. However, in all cases, you should concentrate on making notes of the main points before writing your final version. You may, of course, use all of these passages to practise writing more conventional summaries of their content if you wish. Whatever approach you follow, remember to use your own words as far as possible and to write between 200–250 words, apart from Exercise 4 which should be between 300–350 words (and can also be used as the basis for a practice task for directed writing questions). The following exercises are suitable for both Core/ Foundation and Extended/Higher Curriculum students to use for practice.

Exercise 1

Read carefully the following passage. Then imagine that you are a television news reporter who was present when this speech was given. Write the words of your report to the viewers in which you make clear the attitude of the speaker and his beliefs about modern education.

Why Schools Don't Educate

By John Taylor Gatto

I've noticed a fascinating phenomenon in my twenty-five years of teaching – that schools and schooling are increasingly irrelevant to the great enterprises of the planet. No one believes anymore that scientists are trained in science classes or politicians in civics classes or poets in English classes. The truth is that schools don't really teach anything except how to obey orders. This is a great mystery to me because thousands of humane, caring people work in schools as teachers and aides and administrators but the abstract logic of the institution overwhelms their individual contributions. Although teachers do care and do work very hard, the institution is psychopathic – it has no conscience. It rings a bell and the young man in the middle of writing a poem must close his notebook and move to a different cell where he must memorize that man and monkeys derive from a common ancestor.

It is absurd and anti-life to be part of a system that compels you to sit in confinement with people of exactly the same age and social class. That system effectively cuts you off from the immense diversity of life and the synergy of variety, indeed it cuts you off from your own past and future, scaling you to a continuous present much the same way television does.

It is absurd and anti-life to be part of a system that compels you to listen to a stranger reading poetry when you want to learn to construct buildings, or to sit with a stranger discussing the construction of buildings when you want to read poetry.

It is absurd and anti-life to move from cell to cell at the sound of a gong for every day of your natural youth in an institution that allows you no privacy and even follows you into the sanctuary of your home demanding that you do its 'homework'.

How will they learn to read? My answer is [that] when children are given whole lives instead of age-graded ones in cellblocks, they learn to read, write, and do arithmetic with ease, if those things make sense in the kind of life that unfolds around them.

But keep in mind that in the United States almost nobody who reads, writes or does arithmetic gets much respect. We are a land of talkers, we pay talkers the most and admire talkers the most, and so our children talk constantly, following the public models of television and schoolteachers. It is very difficult to teach the 'basics' anymore because they really aren't basic to the society we've made.

Two institutions at present control our children's lives – television and schooling, in that order. Both of these reduce the real world of wisdom, fortitude, temperance, and justice to a never-ending, non-stopping abstraction. In centuries past, the time of a child and adolescent would be occupied in real work, real charity, real adventures, and the realistic search for mentors who might teach what you really wanted to learn. A great deal of time was spent in community pursuits, practising affection, meeting and studying every level of the community, learning how to make a home, and dozens of other tasks necessary to become a whole man or woman.

From The Natural Child Project

Exercise 2

By referring closely to the following passage explain, using your own words:

● what you have learned about Mrs Jellyby and the house in which she lives
● the specific criticisms that the author is making of her and her lifestyle. (Note: in this part of the question you are asked to describe the author's criticisms, not to summarise the comments made by the character in the novel who is describing the visit.)

MRS JELLYBY

I therefore supposed that Mrs Jellyby was not at home; and was quite surprised when the person appeared in the passage without the pattens [wooden shoes], and going up to the back room on the first floor, before Ada and me, announced us as, 'Them two young ladies, Missis Jellyby!' We passed several more children on the way up, whom it was difficult to avoid treading on in the dark; and as we came into Mrs Jellyby's presence, one of the poor little things fell down-stairs – down a whole flight (as it sounded to me), with a great noise.

Mrs Jellyby, whose face reflected none of the uneasiness which we could not help showing in our own faces, as the dear child's head recorded its passage with a bump on every stair – Richard afterwards said he counted seven, besides one for the landing – received us with perfect equanimity. She was a pretty, very diminutive, plump woman of from forty to fifty, with handsome eyes, though they had a curious habit of seeming to look a long way off. As if – I am quoting Richard again – they could see nothing nearer than Africa!

'I am very glad indeed,' said Mrs Jellyby in an agreeable voice, 'to have the pleasure of receiving you. I have a great respect for Mr Jarndyce, and no one in whom he is interested can be an object of indifference to me.'

We expressed our acknowledgments, and sat down behind the door where there was a lame invalid of a sofa. Mrs Jellyby had very good hair, but was too much occupied with her African duties to brush it. The shawl in which she had been loosely muffled, dropped on to her chair when she advanced to us; and as she turned to resume her seat, we could not help noticing that her dress didn't nearly meet up the back, and that the open space was railed across with a lattice-work of stay-lace – like a summer-house.

The room, which was strewn with papers and nearly filled by a great writing-table covered with similar litter, was, I must say, not only very untidy but very dirty. We were obliged to take notice of that with our sense of sight, even while, with our sense of hearing, we followed the poor child who had tumbled down-stairs: I think into the back kitchen, where somebody seemed to stifle him.

But what principally struck us was a jaded and unhealthy-looking, though by no means plain girl, at the writing-table, who sat biting the feather of her pen, and staring at us. I suppose nobody ever was in such a state of ink. And, from her tumbled hair to her pretty feet, which were disfigured with frayed and broken satin slippers trodden down at heel, she really seemed to have no article of dress upon her, from a pin upwards, that was in its proper condition or its right place.

> 'You find me, my dears,' said Mrs Jellyby, snuffing the two great office candles in tin candlesticks which made the room taste strongly of hot tallow (the fire had gone out, and there was nothing in the grate but ashes, a bundle of wood, and a poker), 'you find me, my dears, as usual, very busy; but that you will excuse. The African project at present employs my whole time. It involves me in correspondence with public bodies, and with private individuals anxious for the welfare of their species all over the country. I am happy to say it is advancing. We hope by this time next year to have from a hundred and fifty to two hundred healthy families cultivating coffee and educating the natives of Borrioboola-Gha, on the left bank of the Niger.'
>
> From *Bleak House* by Charles Dickens

Exercise 3

Read carefully the following passage. Then write a summary of the key points about the origins of advertising for a textbook intended for school students in Grade 6 (10–11 years old).

Early Advertising

Although word of mouth, the most basic (and still the most powerful) form of advertising, has been around ever since humans started providing each other with goods and services, Advertising as a discrete form is generally agreed to have begun alongside newspapers, in the seventeenth century. Frenchman Théophraste Renaudot (Louis XIII's official physician) created a very early version of the supermarket noticeboard, a 'bureau des addresses et des rencontres'. Parisians seeking or offering jobs, or wanting to buy or sell goods, put notices at the office on Île de la Cité. So that the maximum number of people had access to this information, Renaudot created La Gazette in 1631, the first French newspaper. The personal ad was born.

In England, line advertisements in newspapers were very popular in the second half of the seventeenth century, often announcing the publication of a new book, or the opening of a new play. The Great Fire of London in 1666 was a boost to this type of advertisement, as people used newspapers in the aftermath of the fire to advertise lost and found, and changes of address. These early line ads were predominantly informative, containing descriptive, rather than persuasive language.

Advertisements were of key importance, even at this early point in their history, when it came to informing consumers about new products. Coffee is one such example. Coffee was first brewed into a drink in the Middle East, in the fifteenth century. The Arabs kept the existence of this vivifying concoction a secret, refusing to export beans (or instructions on how to grind and brew them). Legend has it that Sufi Baba Budan smuggled seven beans into India in 1570 and planted them. Coffee then spread to Italy, and throughout Europe, served at coffeehouses. The rapid spread of coffee as both a drink and a pattern of behaviour (coffeehouses became social gathering places) is in no small part due to the advertising of coffee's benefits in newspapers.

When goods were hand-made, by local craftsmen, in small quantities, there was no need for advertising. Buyer and seller were personally known to one another, and the buyer was likely to have direct experience of the product. The buyer also had much more contact with the production process, especially for items like clothing (hand-stitched to fit) and food (assembled from simple, raw ingredients). Packaging and branding were unknown and unnecessary before the Industrial Revolution. However, once technological advances enabled the mass production

►►

of soap, china, clothing, etc., the close personal links between buyer and seller were broken. Rather than selling out of their back yards to local customers, manufacturers sought markets a long way from their factories, sometimes on the other side of the world.

This created a need for advertising. Manufacturers needed to explain and recommend their products to customers whom they would never meet personally. Manufacturers, in chasing far-off markets, were beginning to compete with each other. Therefore they needed to **brand** their products, in order to distinguish them from one another, and create mass recommendations to support the mass production and consumption model.

Newspapers provided the ideal vehicle for this new phenomenon, advertisements. New technologies were also making newspapers cheaper, more widely available, and more frequently printed. They had more pages, so they could carry more, bigger, advertisements. Simple descriptions, plus prices, of products served their purpose until the mid-nineteenth century, when technological advances meant that illustrations could be added to advertising, and colour was also an option. Advertisers started to add **copy** under the simple headings, describing their products using persuasive prose.

An early advertising success story is that of Pears Soap. Thomas Barratt married into the famous soap-making family and realised that they needed to be more aggressive about pushing their products if they were to survive. He bought the copyright to a painting by noted Pre-Raphaelite artist, Sir John Everett Millais, originally entitled 'Bubbles'. Barratt added a bar of Pears Soap to the bottom left of the image, and emblazoned the company name across the top, launching the series of ads featuring cherubic children which firmly welded the brand to the values it still holds today. He took images considered as 'fine art' and used them to connote his brand's quality, purity (i.e. untainted by commercialism) and simplicity (cherubic children). The campaign was a huge success.

Taken from *Mediaknowall*

Exercise 4

Read carefully the two passages that follow. Then imagine that you have visited Efteling Theme Park with your family (including a younger sister) while on holiday in Europe. Using details from both passages, write the words for a web blog intended for your friends at home. In your blog:

- give a brief description of the park
- describe what you did there
- say what you and your sister enjoyed and did not enjoy.

Visit to Efteling Theme Park

One of our fun-filled outings as a family with young kids has been to Efteling Theme Park, in the Netherlands. Efteling is one of the oldest theme parks in the world (rumour has it that the Disney Parks have been inspired by Efteling). It is a fantasy-based theme park and all rides and attractions are based on popular fairy tales, folklores, myths and legends. As you enter the parking lot the building with its pointed cones beckons you with promises and treats galore. Once you get inside, both children and adults are transported to a totally charming land of fairy tale characters and interesting rides.

The park is based over an area of 160 acres (about 0.6 km²) and spread over a natural forest area with pine trees and many ponds and gardens which have been all used scenically to create an old world charm making it very different from a modern theme park. What I also want to say is there is a fair bit of walking to do. One can take prams for little ones or can even rent some push-cars for the older ones. You can also take a steam train from a quaint station which takes you around the park and its attractions.

Efteling started in 1952 as a theme park for children and then kept adding incrementally to become a park targeted at both adults and children. The entire park can be divided into 4 realms broadly speaking – Fairy, Travel, Adventure and Other Realm (names make more sense in Dutch, but presenting the English translations here) – based on the type of attractions.

If you go with young ones, you are most likely to do the Fairy Realm in detail, which is what we did in the half day we had there. Wander into the Fairy Tale Forest and encounter fairy-tale characters – Rapunzel lowering her hair, the dancing red shoes, the houses of Rumpelstiltskin, Snow White and the seven dwarfs, The Frog King, Sleeping Beauty, Long-Neck, etc. Most of these are houses which show the characters with all the props and the attention to detail is really commendable. The most compelling of the lot was the Fairy Tale Tree (Sprookjesboom).The tree tells all those gathered around it fairy tales and you can almost believe it's true as you see it moving its jaws. There are also these waste paper bins called Holle Bolle Gijs, based on the story of a very hungry boy, who keeps saying paper here, paper here, basically meaning don't litter.

A must-see is Efteling Museum which also tells us about the history of the Park, a pity most of it is in Dutch. My personal favorite was the Diorama – a 3D miniature model of railways, houses, lives of the fairy-tale people. I also loved Villa Volta – a madhouse where you experience bizarre things. Raveleijn is a live animation show, based on a fantasy book for young children. There is a Steam Carousel which is popular, too.

I would say that it's impossible to do the entire park in one day, or half a day. There is an option to stay in the park in a hotel or outside in other hotels in Kaastheuvel, which gives you an option of starting early and exploring more. There are many options for food – also for vegetarians. If you are ever in the Netherlands or Belgium, do plan to visit this park.

The Fairy Tale Tree

Adapted from *Indian Moms Connect*, 2 January 2013

Cheesy ... but charming

Sheryl Garratt

Sheryl Garratt and five-year-old son Liam visit an eccentric Dutch theme park. No Mickey Mouse here – it's more fairies and trolls, snowball-throwing games and talking litter bins ...

Soon after arriving at the Dutch theme park, Efteling, we were in a boat on a man-made waterway which is pretty much as you'd expect of a trip to Holland. Apart from the camels and the crocodiles ...

Floating through the bazaar of the fictional Arabian town of Fata Morgana, we passed hordes of shoppers and beggars crowding the bazaar while a man screamed in agony as a dentist administered to him in an open-air surgery. We even got to drift between the legs of a giant.

An hour or so later, we were floating again, this time in the air in open-fronted cable cars. The fairytale scenes before us on the Dream Flight were cheesy but charming, and beautifully done: the smells and temperature changed as we moved from one set to another; fairies perched in trees in a rainy wood full of goblins and trolls.

These state-of-the-art rides are recent additions to a fairy tale-themed park that is almost 50 years old, set in the Brabant region near the Belgian border. Efteling's mature woods make it less artificial than most theme parks, with clever details like talking litter bins to keep little minds occupied and little legs walking. Wholesome and quietly appealing, it's a great place to blow away the winter cobwebs.

My five-year-old son's favourite spot was the Fairytale Forest, featuring low-tech tableaux from various fairy stories. A fakir who was charming tulips from the ground before flying from one side of his home to another on a creaky magic carpet had Liam transfixed.

We stayed in the Efteling Hotel, well suited for children. It has a generous play area with actors dressed as fairies and trolls. The family rooms were large and comfortable and the hotel has its own entrance to the park, allowing guests to get to some of the more popular rides before queues build up.

The next morning, my husband played with our son in a nearby maze, whilst I rode on the stomach-churning Bird Rok, an indoor rollercoaster which lurches around for much of the time in total darkness, leaving you disorientated. 'Mum, you look funny,' observed Liam cheerfully as I got off; ignoring my pale smile he dragged me on to the nearby Carnival Festival ride. He loved it and wanted to go on again immediately.

This is only the second year the park has opened during the winter months, as 'Winter' Efteling. Although the majority of the rollercoasters and white-knuckle rides are closed, and can be seen only from the carriages of a steam train which chugs around the park, there is plenty added on to compensate. There's a huge indoor skating rink, where small children glide along holding on to chairs and parents can have hot drinks in the 'après-ski' bar. An indoor winter wonderland playground provides huge inflatables, snowball-throwing stalls and a snow slide that children can hurtle down on tyres.

On the crisp, clear winter days we were there, we were warmed up by frequent visits to reasonably priced stalls selling hot chocolate and delicious hot snacks (from doughnuts to French fries with mayonnaise). However, there is plenty to do undercover, so even rain wouldn't have dampened our spirits. We spent more than an hour, for instance, in a building housing a glorious 150-year-old steam carousel, an ornate miniature railway, a theatre where fountains danced to music and several refreshment bars.

Adapted from the *Observer*, 25 November 2001

Becoming a better writer

This chapter gives you some key guidelines and principles about writing which are relevant to any kind of writing task. Whatever piece of writing you try, you need to **think about its purpose** and decide what effect this has on your writing style. There are two key questions to ask yourself:

- **What is it for?** In other words, what kind of writing piece is it (it could be anything from a fantasy story to a business letter) and what do you want to say? You need to be able to **use different styles for different purposes**.
- **Who is it for?** Who are the readers for this piece of writing? You need to be able to **use different styles for different audiences**.

Even when we think about just one kind of writing task – a letter – the style will need to be different depending on who the letter is for (a relative? a newspaper? a friend?). When you write an article you need to think about your readers: if it is for a group of young people, for instance, you need to think about how to make it clear and interesting for them, not just about what information you want to include.

● Different styles for different purposes

Writing to inform or explain

This kind of writing is factual and the important thing is for it to be as clear as possible, whether you are explaining a situation, an activity or an interest, or providing some instructions for carrying out a task. Make sure your writing is **focused and objective**, **clear and systematic**.

Be focused and objective

Your purpose is to make the information clear to your readers, not to give them your own opinion on the subject, so stick closely to the subject and don't be tempted to add comments of your own.

Be clear and systematic

The point of an explanation is that it should be simpler and clearer than the original. Here are some techniques to help you achieve this.

- Use vocabulary that is easy to understand.
- If you are answering a directed writing question, be careful not simply to repeat chunks of the original text; instead, find simpler ways to express the same ideas so that you are genuinely explaining them.
- Use sentences that are not too long or complicated.
- Make sure your punctuation is accurate and helpful so that readers can easily see their way from one point to the next.
- Use a new paragraph for every main point that you make: start the paragraph with a 'topic sentence' to tell your reader what the paragraph will be about and use the rest of the paragraph to develop the point.

Example of informative writing

Sports injuries

Sports-related injuries occur when sportsmen and women either fail to warm up properly, over-train, use incorrect equipment or adopt a faulty technique. Injuries may also follow an accident or foul play. Injuries to soft tissues, including muscles and tendons, are very common and lead to pain and various degrees of immobility. Fortunately, many sports-related injuries can be prevented by observing a few simple measures such as warming up and cooling down properly, using the proper equipment and correct techniques.

Common sports injuries

Ankle sprain

Ankle sprain: caused by tearing the ligament fibres that support the ankle when the foot turns over onto its outer edge. An ankle sprain may occur in many different types of sport, but it is commonly associated with badminton, football, squash and tennis.

Pulled hamstring

Pulled hamstring: caused by tearing the muscle fibre at the back of the thigh as a result of overstretching. A pulled hamstring often occurs while sprinting or kicking a ball.

Torn cartilage

Torn cartilage: caused by a sudden twisting movement while the knee is bent and subject to the full weight of the body. Footballers, rugby players and skiers are particularly prone to cartilage trouble.

Tendonitis

Tendonitis: inflammation of a tendon at the back of the heel. Various causes include long-distance running shoes (wearing new running shoes, wearing running shoes that do not support the heel) and change of normal running surface.

Tenosynovitis

Tenosynovitis (inflammation of tendon linings): commonly occurs in the wrist, caused by the overuse of muscles. Any racket sport may lead participants to use a vulnerable, powerful grip, e.g. rowing and weightlifting. Contributory factors include using the wrong size handle or a faulty technique when gripping the racket, oar or bar.

Shin splints

Shin splints: caused by strained tendons or muscles in the front of the lower leg when walking or running. This results in pain around the shin area that eases off when resting. Shin splints are associated with unusual or abnormal foot posture.

Bruises

Bruises (contusions): occur when an injury causes bleeding from blood capillaries beneath the skin. This leads to discoloration under the surface. Bruises arise following a blunt blow such as a punch or kick and may appear hours, or even days after an injury.

Blisters

Blisters form on skin that has been damaged by friction or heat. Tissue fluid leaks into the affected area forming a 'bubble'. Never deliberately burst a blister as this may lead to infection. Should the blister break, cover it with a dry, non-stick dressing. Otherwise, leave a blister to heal on its own and cover with a special protective blister plaster.

From UniChem Pharmacies

This piece of informative writing is in the form of a leaflet. Points are made under clear headings. In a continuous piece of writing, such headings would not be necessary, but here they aid understanding.

Technical terms for injuries are explained in straightforward vocabulary.

Sentences tend to be short, each dealing with a single point.

Here each section is separated by a heading, but note that the colon is used to good effect to clarify.

Each paragraph begins with a topic sentence and the rest of the paragraph elaborates, giving examples to illustrate.

Writing to argue or persuade

This kind of writing needs to be **convincing and logical**. Here are some useful techniques.

- Decide **what** you want to persuade your reader to believe. Which viewpoint are you going to put forward?
- Make 'for and against' lists: one list of the facts and ideas from the text which support your viewpoint, and another list of those which do not. Note: you can change your chosen viewpoint at this planning stage, but don't change it as you are writing!
- State your chosen viewpoint simply at the beginning.
- For each main point that you make to support your viewpoint, **give evidence and examples** to back up your case – **use the text!**
- **Be balanced** – your argument will be at its most convincing if you make points for both sides but prove that your own chosen viewpoint is the better one. Use your 'for and against' lists.
- Use paragraphs to help you make your points clearly. Start a new paragraph for each main point that you make and use the rest of the paragraph to give your evidence. This will mean that your paragraphs are of roughly similar lengths.
- Use persuasive phrases such as: 'It seems clear to me that …', 'The text shows that …', 'This example indicates that …'.
- Use linking phrases to move between the two sides of the argument, such as: 'Nevertheless, …', 'On the other hand, …'.
- Rhetorical questions are a good way to get your reader on your side: these are questions which have an obvious answer, and the answer supports your point of view! For example, if you were arguing against animal experiments, you could ask: 'Would you like your own pets to have shampoo squirted into their eyes?' If you were arguing in favour of animal experiments, you could ask: 'Your little brother is dangerously ill – would you rather he had drugs whose safety had been tested on animals, or no drugs?'
- Finish by restating your viewpoint, perhaps saying also that although you can see the other point of view, you are convinced that yours is the right one.

Example of persuasive writing

School uniforms: turning our kids into soulless conformists

It would seem that nowadays, every educationalist is a fan of the dreaded blazer/tie school uniform combo. The journalist, Suzanne Moore, questions exactly how do they really think they're helping prepare schoolchildren for the 'real world'?

Unsurprisingly, I was never a fan of my own school uniform, which was bottle-green in colour. We were constantly lectured about the activities we were not allowed to be seen doing in it. In

▶▶

a hazy way, I remember them as basically eating chips and talking to boys. 'I'll just take it off then, Miss,' I used to say, for I was annoying then as I am now.

The price of the uniform itself was an issue. The wear and tear of it was an issue. We couldn't afford it. Once I had a Saturday job that helped, but naturally I bought myself some lime-green plastic platform shoes. Weirdly they were not acceptable as school shoes unless my mum wrote a note. What medical condition required the wearing of these beauties I can only guess, but my mum's notes I now look on with awe, the end line nearly always being: 'She is in a phase.'

Did this uniform instil in me a sense of oneness with my school? Did it resolve the class issue? Er ... not exactly. In those days we didn't have stupid fashion words like 'vintage' and 'pre-loved', we had hand-me-downs, and really, I don't know a modern child who wants a second-hand uniform.

The myth of uniform is that it is a social leveller, an equaliser. And pushes up results? Then show me how. Many European countries with good schools don't have uniforms. Bill Clinton thought back in the 90s that it might be the answer to gang-related violence. It wasn't.

No, uniform does what it says on the tin. It is about conforming. It heartens many a parent to see their child as somehow ready for work. Politicians love a uniform. Indeed the fetishisation of school uniform is education policy. Most schools are obsessed with it, parents like it and many children say it makes their lives easier.

Teachers vary, some reporting that too much of their time is spent on policing clothing violations. If education is to be about conforming and not drawing out talent, I guess that's fine, though the kind of overall worn in France for science or art would surely suffice. Uniform covers up many social ills. Sometimes, even poor parenting. ('Well they were always clean and in the right uniform.') The signifiers of class and money are simply rejigged around bags, phone and pens. It is as it ever was.

This nostalgia for a uniform is based on emotion not reason. Evidence does not come into it. Does all this produce better results? Happier children? What we really have, alongside the increasing prevalence of the ghastly blazer/tie combo, is increasing social inequality. You could map it out but don't ask me to, as I missed an awful lot of school on account of this kind of attitude. 'Don't ask questions, girl, and put your tie on properly.'

Don't ask questions about the world of work that we are preparing children for. At the moment it looks as if some will work for free in some superstore uniform. Get them used to it early. Compliance. Zero tolerance. The best days of your life.

The final three paragraphs return to the writer's own experiences which are those shared by many of her readers. This technique gives the whole argument more weight and authenticity.

The final paragraph starts quite light-heartedly with the statement that the writer's daughter appears to be proud of her uniform (and, not surprisingly, is perhaps doing this to 'get at' her mother). However, the

> My daughter will shortly start at a new school and in the Uniform Me shop this week it was hot and sweaty, as nasty polo shirts were pulled on. Skirts must be knee-length with over-the-knee socks. At least the stuff I bought was cheap. Some inner-city uniforms are close to $300.
>
> When I have had jobs where I had to wear a uniform – in restaurants and hospitals – I just got on with it. I saw the need. But to learn? To learn what? Again, I ask: where is the evidence that uniform works?
>
> Since I bought my daughter's uniform she has, of course, had it on all the time, though school doesn't start until next week. She is expressing herself or getting at me. She makes me laugh. But the idea saddens me that when she gets to secondary school individuality must be knocked out of her as early as possible via the reinforcement of petty rules about shirts. This is indeed preparation for the real world. Of uniform thinking.
>
> Adapted from the *Guardian*, 29 August 2012

tone becomes more serious at the end and the writer leaves us with a thought to reflect upon. This is given extra force by being expressed as a three-word, short sentence without a main verb.

Note the use of vocabulary:
• 'myth' (which suggests that there is no substance to the requirement to wear a uniform)
• 'fetishisation' – a word that conveys the idea that there is something unnatural and perverse about the idea of wearing a uniform.
Note the beginnings of sentences which engage the reader and link ideas:
• Unsurprisingly, …
• No uniform does what it says on the tin.
• Don't ask questions about the world of work …
• When I have had jobs where I have had to wear a uniform …

Writing imaginatively to entertain your readers

If you are writing an imaginative piece – narrating a story, for example – you will not have to structure your piece in the same logical, argued way as for an informative or persuasive piece. However, it is still important that your writing has a clear structure. Perhaps most importantly, you need to know how your story will end before you start (see the section on planning on pages 64–67). You might want your ending to be a surprise to your readers, but it shouldn't be a surprise to you! The beginning is important, too. For a story you can either:

● start by setting the scene – this is fine, but don't give too much time/space to it, keep it to one short paragraph
● go straight into the story, for example with a line of dialogue.

A good piece of imaginative writing is **varied and inventive**. Here are some ideas on how to make sure your skills in this area are clear to the reader!

Be varied and inventive

● Use some words which are abstract and colourful.
● Use descriptive vocabulary: adjectives, adverbs.
● Use imagery, for example, 'she grinned like a crocodile'.
● Use exclamations and/or words that convey their meaning through sound. (These might be dramatic, for example, 'Thud!', 'Crash!'; or they might just be well-chosen words that convey the exact sound you have in mind, for example, 'tinkling', 'rustled'.)
● Your paragraphs should vary in length. An occasional very short paragraph can make a strong impact. Some paragraphs might even be just one word long, such as 'Help!'
● Your sentences should also vary in length – this is a good way to have an effect on your reader's feelings. For example, if you have just been setting a frightening scene, a short sentence such as 'We waited.' or even just 'Silence.' can be very effective.

Example of imaginative writing

FLIGHT

A short story by Doris Lessing

Above the old man's head was the dovecote, a tall wire-netted shelf on stilts, full of strutting, preening birds. The sunlight broke on their grey breasts into small rainbows. His ears were lulled by their crooning, his hands stretched up towards his favourite, a homing pigeon, a young plump-bodied bird which stood still when it saw him and cocked a shrewd bright eye.

'Pretty, pretty, pretty,' he said, as he grasped the bird and drew it down, feeling the cold coral claws tighten around his finger. Content, he rested the bird lightly on his chest, and leaned against a tree, gazing out beyond the dovecote into the landscape of a late afternoon. In folds and hollows of sunlight and shade, the dark red soil, which was broken into great dusty clods, stretched wide to a tall horizon. Trees marked the course of the valley; a stream of rich green grass the road.

His eyes travelled homewards along this road until he saw his grand-daughter swinging on the gate underneath a frangipani tree. Her hair fell down her back in a wave of sunlight, and her long bare legs repeated the angles of the frangipani stems, bare, shining-brown stems among patterns of pale blossoms.

She was gazing past the pink flowers, past the railway cottage where they lived, along the road to the village.

His mood shifted. He deliberately held out his wrist for the bird to take flight, and caught it again at the moment it spread its wings. He felt the plump shape strive and strain under his fingers; and, in a sudden access of troubled spite, shut the bird into a small box and fastened the bolt. 'Now you stay there,' he muttered; and turned his back on the shelf of birds. He moved warily along the hedge, stalking his grand-daughter, who was now looped over the gate, her head loose on her arms, singing.

The light happy sound mingled with the crooning of the birds, and his anger mounted.

You will see that the paragraphs are of varied lengths, some of them very short.

Metaphor is used to enhance the description effectively – 'Her hair fell down her back in a wave of sunlight'.

Notice the skilfully controlled use of direct speech, which adds immediacy to the story and engages the reader.

'Hey!' he shouted; saw her jump, look back, and abandon the gate. Her eyes veiled themselves, and she said in a pert neutral voice: 'Hullo, Grandad.' Politely she moved towards him, after a lingering backward glance at the road.

'Waiting for Steven, hey?' he said, his fingers curling like claws into his palm.

'Any objection?' she asked lightly, refusing to look at him.

He confronted her, his eyes narrowed, shoulders hunched, tight in a hard knot of pain which included the preening birds, the sunlight, the flowers. He said: 'Think you're old enough to go courting, hey?'

The girl tossed her head at the old-fashioned phrase and sulked. 'Oh, Grandad!'

'Think you want to leave home, hey? Think you can go running around the fields at night?'

Her smile made him see her, as he had every evening of this warm end-of-summer month, swinging hand in hand along the road to the village with that red-handed, red-throated, violent-bodied youth, the son of the postmaster. Misery went to his head and he shouted angrily: 'I'll tell your mother!'

'Tell away!' she said, laughing, and went back to the gate.

He heard – her singing, for him to hear:

'I've got you under my skin,

I've got you deep in the heart of ...'

'Rubbish,' he shouted. 'Rubbish. Impudent little bit of rubbish!'

Growling under his breath he turned towards the dovecote, which was his refuge from the house he shared with his daughter and her husband and their children. But now the house would be empty. Gone all the young girls with their laughter and their squabbling and their teasing. He would be left, uncherished and alone, with that square-fronted, calm-eyed woman, his daughter.

He stooped, muttering, before the dovecote, resenting the absorbed cooing birds.

From the gate the girl shouted: 'Go and tell! Go on, what are you waiting for?'

Obstinately he made his way to the house, with quick, pathetic persistent glances of appeal back at her. But she never looked around. Her defiant but anxious young body stung him into love and repentance. He stopped. 'But I never meant ...' he muttered, waiting for her to turn and run to him. 'I didn't mean ...'

She did not turn. She had forgotten him. Along the road came the young man Steven, with something in his hand. A present for her? The old man stiffened as he watched the gate swing back, and the couple embrace. In the brittle shadows of the frangipani tree his grand-daughter, his darling, lay in the arms of the postmaster's son, and her hair flowed back over his shoulder.

'I see you!' shouted the old man spitefully. They did not move. He stumped into the little whitewashed house, hearing the wooden veranda creak angrily under his feet. His daughter was sewing in the front room, threading a needle held to the light.

He stopped again, looking back into the garden. The couple were now sauntering among the bushes, laughing. As he watched he saw the girl escape from the youth with a sudden mischievous movement, and run off through the flowers with him in pursuit. He heard shouts, laughter, a scream, silence.

'But it's not like that at all,' he muttered miserably. 'It's not like that. Why can't you see? Running and giggling, and kissing and kissing. You'll come to something quite different.'

He looked at his daughter with sardonic hatred, hating himself. They were caught and finished, both of them, but the girl was still running free.

'Can't you *see*?' he demanded of his invisible grand-daughter, who was at that moment lying in the thick green grass with the postmaster's son.

His daughter looked at him and her eyebrows went up in tired forbearance.

'Put your birds to bed?' she asked, humouring him.

'Lucy,' he said urgently. 'Lucy …'

'Well what is it now?'

'She's in the garden with Steven.'

'Now you just sit down and have your tea.'

He stumped his feet alternately, thump, thump, on the hollow wooden floor and shouted: 'She'll marry him. I'm telling you, she'll be marrying him next!'

His daughter rose swiftly, brought him a cup, set him a plate.

'I don't want any tea. I don't want it, I tell you.'

'Now, now,' she crooned. 'What's wrong with it? Why not?'

'She's eighteen. Eighteen!'

'I was married at seventeen and I never regretted it.'

'Liar,' he said. 'Liar. Then you should regret it. Why do you make your girls marry? It's you who do it. What do you do it for? Why?'

'The other three have done fine. They've three fine husbands. Why not Alice?'

'She's the last,' he mourned. 'Can't we keep her a bit longer?'

'Come, now, dad. She'll be down the road, that's all. She'll be here every day to see you.'

'But it's not the same.' He thought of the other three girls, transformed inside a few months from charming petulant spoiled children into serious young matrons.

'You never did like it when we married?' she said. 'Why not? Every time, it's the same. When I got married you made me feel like it was something wrong. And my girls the same. You get them all crying and miserable the way you go on. Leave Alice alone. She's happy.' She sighed, letting her eyes linger on the sun-lit garden. 'She'll marry next month. There's no reason to wait.'

'You've said they can marry?' he said incredulously.

'Yes, dad, why not?' she said coldly, and took up her sewing.

His eyes stung, and he went out on to the veranda. Wet spread down over his chin and he took out a handkerchief and mopped his whole face. The garden was empty.

From around a corner came the young couple; but their faces were no longer set against him. On the wrist of the postmaster's son balanced a young pigeon, the light gleaming on its breast.

'For me?' said the old man, letting the drops shake off his chin. 'For me?'

'Do you like it?' The girl grabbed his hand and swung on it. 'It's for you, Grandad. Steven brought it for you.' They hung about him, affectionate,

There is creation of sound through the use of short words and repetition – 'He stumped his feet alternately, thump, thump, on the hollow wooden floor.'

concerned, trying to charm away his wet eyes and his misery. They took his arms and directed him to the shelf of birds, one on each side, enclosing him, petting him, saying wordlessly that nothing would be changed, nothing could change, and that they would be with him always. The bird was proof of it, they said, from their lying happy eyes, as they thrust it on him. 'There, Grandad, it's yours. It's for you.'

They watched him as he held it on his wrist, stroking its soft, sun-warmed back, watching the wings lift and balance.

'You must shut it up for a bit,' said the girl intimately. 'Until it knows this is its home.'

'Teach your grandmother to suck eggs,' growled the old man.

Released by his half-deliberate anger, they fell back, laughing at him. 'We're glad you like it.' They moved off, now serious and full of purpose, to the gate, where they hung, backs to him, talking quietly. More than anything could, their grown-up seriousness shut him out, making him alone; also, it quietened him, took the sting out of their tumbling like puppies on the grass. They had forgotten him again. Well, so they should, the old man reassured himself, feeling his throat clotted with tears, his lips trembling. He held the new bird to his face, for the caress of its silken feathers. Then he shut it in a box and took out his favourite.

'*Now* you can go,' he said aloud. He held it poised, ready for flight, while he looked down the garden towards the boy and the girl. Then, clenched in the pain of loss, he lifted the bird on his wrist, and watched it soar. A whirr and a spatter of wings, and a cloud of birds rose into the evening from the dovecote.

At the gate Alice and Steven forgot their talk and watched the birds.

On the veranda, that woman, his daughter, stood gazing, her eyes shaded with a hand that still held her sewing.

It seemed to the old man that the whole afternoon had stilled to watch his gesture of self-command, that even the leaves of the trees had stopped shaking.

Dry-eyed and calm, he let his hands fall to his sides and stood erect, staring up into the sky.

The cloud of shining silver birds flew up and up, with a shrill cleaving of wings, over the dark ploughed land and the darker belts of trees and the bright folds of grass, until they floated high in the sunlight, like a cloud of motes of dust.

They wheeled in a wide circle, tilting their wings so there was flash after flash of light, and one after another they dropped from the sunshine of the upper sky to shadow, one after another, returning to the shadowed earth over trees and grass and field, returning to the valley and the shelter of night.

The garden was all a fluster and a flurry of returning birds. Then silence, and the sky was empty.

The old man turned, slowly, taking his time; he lifted his eyes to smile proudly down the garden at his grand-daughter. She was staring at him. She did not smile. She was wide-eyed, and pale in the cold shadow, and he saw the tears run shivering off her face.

From *The Habit of Loving*, by Doris Lessing, Flamingo, 1993

The writer varies the paragraph length in order to convey the changing pace of the action.

Decide for yourself how effectively the end of the story works and what the link is between the grandfather, grand-daughter and the pigeons.

● Different styles for different audiences

Who are you writing for?

Now that we have looked at the purpose of your writing, or **what** you are writing for, it's important to think about your **audience**, or **who you are writing for**. It is important that you use language and register appropriate to audience and context.

When you are writing in an examination, in one sense your audience is always one adult – the person who will mark the paper. However, sometimes for a particular writing task you will also be required to consider another specific audience, for example:

children

a school newspaper

your headteacher

a member of your local community council

It is important to think about your audience and how it should affect the way you write.

- If you are writing for children, the vocabulary you use must be simple, the sentences must be fairly short and they certainly must not be complex.
- If you are writing for your headteacher or to a member of your local community council, then it is appropriate to explore your subject in a more complex or sophisticated way, and to use more difficult or technical vocabulary.

Don't ever start your piece of writing without asking yourself the question 'Who am I writing for?' If your writing shows that you are aware of your audience, you are more likely to gain higher marks.

● Planning your writing

Structuring a piece of writing

The way in which you structure a piece of writing depends on the purpose of the piece and the audience it is being written for.

A structure is likely to go wrong if you don't plan the whole piece of writing before you start. Most importantly, you must know what the end is going to be. If you are writing an argumentative or informative piece, you need to be clear how you are going to balance the argument with points for and against, or how you are going to give one piece of information more prominence than another. If you are writing an imaginative piece, you need to know how you are going to introduce characters and how you are going to describe them, how you are going to create atmosphere and setting, how the plot is going to develop and how your ending is going to work.

On page 70 you will find some comments about paragraphing. Paragraphing is always important but the way you use paragraphs depends on the purpose of your writing. For instance, an argumentative piece will normally be divided into paragraphs of roughly equal length, as an argument has to have a clear and balanced structure. In an imaginative piece the length of the paragraphs will probably be more varied, as the different elements of the narrative will have different degrees of importance.

Generally speaking, the structure should always have the following three parts:

1 Introduction: in a factual piece, this should state **briefly** what the theme of the piece is and – if appropriate – what opinion you are putting forward on this theme. In an imaginative piece, you may choose to set the scene or to go for a more dramatic/immediate start.
2 Main body of explanation/argument/narrative.
3 Conclusion/Story ending.

Practical ways to plan your writing

When writing in an examination, many students are so concerned about finishing in time that it is quite obvious they do not plan their work. This matters, because well-planned writing will almost always score more highly than writing that has not been planned. Whether you are doing a piece of writing in response to a text you have read (see Chapter 3) or a piece of continuous writing for a composition or coursework assignment (see Chapters 6 and 7), it is essential that you plan what you are going to write. There are various methods you can use. **Spider diagrams** and **lists**, as explained in the following pages, are two possibilities, but you may find another method that works best for you.

Spider diagrams
Stage 1

- Write your topic in the middle of the page and around it write down all the things that you might write about.
- At this stage, don't stop to think too much – just write down any relevant ideas that come to mind.

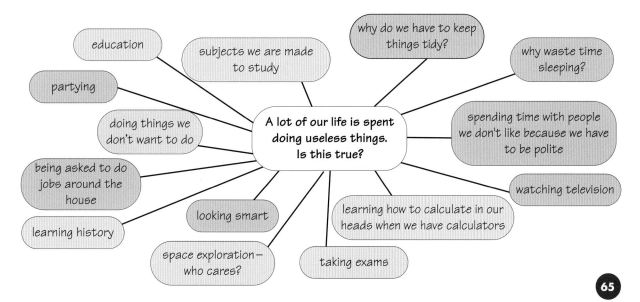

Stage 2

- The next stage is to decide if there are things that need to be discarded, and how to order the points that are being kept.
  - There are a number of points about education (linked by pink lines on the diagram below).
  - There are a number of points about personal life (linked by blue lines).
  - The idea about space exploration is probably going to be discarded.
- Then number the points to give them an order; each numbered point will be a paragraph or part of a paragraph in your composition.

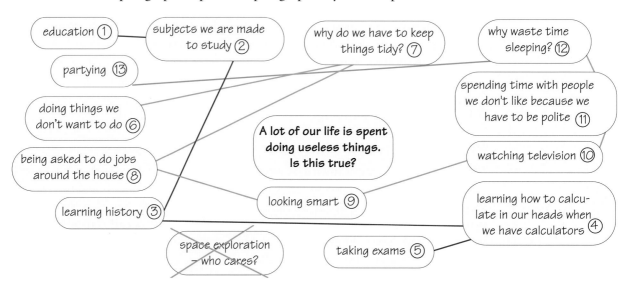

> ## Study tip
>
> 1 At this stage, don't be afraid to cross things out.
> 2 If you find that two of your ideas are closely linked, you should probably combine them.
> 3 Remember that it is not just a case of putting forward one side of the argument – the points being made need to be answered.

Stage 3

The order of the composition now looks like this:

A lot of our life is spent doing useless things. Is this true?

Para 1 General statement about importance of education (1)
Para 2 However – subjects we are made to study are a waste of time. (2) Why learn history? (3) Why bother to learn to do calculations in our heads – calculators! (4)
Para 3 Why do examinations in subjects which are of no importance? (5)
Para 4 General statement about doing things we don't want to do (6)
Para 5 Being pestered to keep our rooms tidy. (7) Doing jobs around the house we don't want to. (8) Being made to look smart when we want to be comfortable. (9)
Para 6 We watch television when we can't think of anything else to do. (10) We spend time with people we don't like (perhaps relatives) because we have to. (11)

Para 7 Why can't someone invent something which means we don't have to waste
time sleeping? (12)
What we want to do is to party (13)
Para 8 Conclusion
What is important in life? What is unimportant?

This might not be how your plan would look in terms of content and ideas.
However, it shows you how you might go about planning.

Why not take the topic title above and do your own plan? You could then go on
to write the composition.

Lists

Instead of a spider diagram, you may prefer simply to put things down in a list.
With this method, it's important to look carefully at the whole list again **before you
start to write**.

- Don't be afraid to change the order of your points.
- Don't automatically think your first ideas are the best: check through the list and
discard/replace some points if you have second thoughts.

However you choose to plan, the crucial point is this: **don't be afraid to spend
time on planning!** If you have an hour to do a piece of writing, you should spend
fifteen minutes planning it. One of the reasons people don't plan is because they
panic about not having enough time. Look on the positive side: if you have a very
clear plan in front of you, you don't have to waste time worrying about what to put
next, so you will write much faster and more efficiently.

● Improving your writing

Always keep in mind the key areas that you are being assessed on for any piece of
writing, whether it is a composition, a piece of directed writing or coursework.
The Cambridge IGCSE First Language English Syllabus states that you should be
able to:

- articulate experience and express what is thought, felt and imagined
- sequence facts, ideas and opinions
- use a range of appropriate vocabulary
- use register appropriate to audience and context
- make accurate use of spelling, punctuation and grammar.

Using Standard English

Languages vary. Each language differs according to the particular area where it is
being spoken, and a language as widespread as English has many different variations
and versions. There are two main kinds of variation:

- accents, which are simply variations in the way the language is pronounced
- dialects, which are more significant variations, each with its own words and
expressions.

The accent and dialect spoken in an area are often an important part of that area's
identity. It is a mistake to say that any particular dialect of a language is 'wrong'
although, in practice, people compare other dialects of English to the form that has
come to be known as Standard English.

The term 'Standard English' is the form of English that is agreed to be generally accepted for written English, and it is the form of the language taught to students learning English. Your written work for any examination testing your English skills should therefore be almost entirely Standard English. This means following some generally recognised Standard English rules about:

- spelling (although US spelling is not penalised in some international examinations)
- punctuation
- paragraphing
- sentence structure.

While written English – for learning purposes, at least – should conform to Standard English, the same does not apply to speech. It would be impossible, for example, to speak in complete sentences all the time – and where are the paragraphs? In speech, language is much less planned and more natural. So, when you are writing in an English Language examination, don't write as you speak *unless* you are writing some words that were spoken or are meant to be spoken, for example:

- when you are quoting someone
- when you are writing direct speech
- when you are writing a script.

Spelling

Some people not only convince themselves that they can't spell but think that, because they can't spell, everything they write is a failure.

The first point to make is that spelling is not the most important thing in the world. If it is a problem for you, look at ways in which you can deal with it. Lack of confidence can make a problem seem worse than it really is. There is no such person as a perfect speller. Everyone makes mistakes from time to time. However, some key strategies can help to improve your spelling, as explained below.

How to improve your spelling

- **Look at words.** People who read a lot see words and absorb them. If you come across a word that you find difficult, pause for a moment and look at it. Look at the shape of the word. After a while you will find that you recognise the word more easily and you can automatically think of its shape.
- **Draw up a list of common words.** Some words occur more frequently in your writing than others. Draw up a list of these words and spend a few minutes each day or every other day reading the list, covering it up and practising writing the words.
- **Learn some spelling rules.** Although there are a lot of words that break rules, nevertheless you can learn rules about spelling which are helpful. 'I before E except after C' for example, helps you spell correctly a whole variety of words that have this letter combination. Find a book on spelling and look up the rules. Don't try to learn them all at once; just try to learn one or two at a time.
- **Say words out loud rather than just staring at the paper.** It won't always mean that you spell them correctly but, if you write down what you hear, the chances are that the word will be recognisable and it might jog your memory.

- **Use a dictionary to check your spelling rather than as the first step**. Don't be discouraged if you can't find the word straight away. Remember, for instance, that some words, such as 'know' and 'gnome', have silent first letters.
- **Make sure you copy out names correctly.** If you are doing a piece of directed writing and there are proper names in the stimulus material, or if you are responding to a piece of literature, there is no excuse for getting the spelling of names of people or places wrong.
- **Remember that vocabulary is more important than spelling.** Don't let uncertainty about spelling frighten you away from using challenging and interesting vocabulary. It is better to use interesting vocabulary with the occasional spelling error than to 'dumb down' your writing, using only very simple words that you know you can spell.
- **Most importantly, remember to check what you have written.** One of the things to check is your spelling. You will probably not correct everything, but increasingly you will find that you can spot your own mistakes.

Punctuation

The first question you should ask yourself when you are thinking about punctuation is, 'What is it for?' Punctuation is all about making life easier for the reader. In particular, it indicates to the reader where he/she needs to pause. There are four punctuation marks that indicate a pause and each indicates a different length of pause.

- The shortest pause is the **comma**. A comma allows you to group words within a longer sentence so that the reader can see the idea developing. If you can, read what you have written out loud. You will find that you naturally pause, and each time you do, put a comma.
- The longest pause is a **full stop**. You put full stops at the ends of sentences. They indicate that the point is complete and finished. Remember that you can't turn simple sentences into more complex ones just by using commas instead of full stops. However short the sentence, once the idea is complete put a full stop.
- In some ways the **semi-colon** is the most difficult of the pause marks to use. When you are reading, look out for semi-colons to see where writers have used them. Read through this book and you will see that we have used semi-colons in several places. If you write a sentence in two balanced halves, and you want to keep the ideas of the two halves together rather than separating them into two sentences, use a semi-colon. The pause is a little longer than a comma and, by using it, you will be saying to the reader 'This is one idea which has two halves'.
- The last of the four pause marks is the **colon**. You use a colon most frequently to introduce a list of items. It allows a substantial pause before the list but doesn't separate everything completely, as a full stop would. (You start a list with a colon and then often use a semi-colon or a comma between the different items on the list.)

Other punctuation marks have specific jobs to do and we will mention two of them here.

- A **question mark** is a specialised full stop – in fact, part of it *is* a full stop. It is used at the end of a sentence that is in the form of a question. It is a signal to the reader that a question has been asked, and that either the next sentence will be in the form of an answer or the reader will be required to think out the answer for him or herself.

- An **exclamation mark** is also used in place of a full stop. It is used at the ends of very short sentences, sometimes one-word sentences, where the writer wants to draw attention to something or pull the reader up short.

You must also know how to punctuate direct speech.

- You put speech marks around the words that are actually spoken.
- Other punctuation marks, such as full stops, commas and question marks, go inside the speech marks.
- Every time speech shifts from one speaker to another, you start a new line.

Remember these points and you won't go far wrong. Don't forget that the purpose of punctuation is to help the reader. Write a paragraph with no punctuation at all and see how difficult it is to read. If you read it aloud, you will notice that you naturally add the punctuation.

Using paragraphs

- A paragraph is a collection of sentences that go together to make a section of a piece of writing. The sentences are all about the same idea.
- The paragraph normally begins with a topic sentence which tells you what the paragraph is going to be about. The other sentences then develop the ideas.
- You could say that paragraphing is a sort of punctuation. A sentence is a group of words that go together to make a sensible whole; a paragraph is a group of sentences that do the same thing.

Make sure not only that you use paragraphs, but that you use them correctly. Sometimes it's easy to forget about paragraphing when you are writing quickly and concentrating on what you want to say. It's important to read through your work to make sure that:

- you have started a new paragraph often enough
- you have started the new paragraphs in sensible places.

Example of clear paragraphing

The short article on pages 71–72 is written in nine paragraphs. You will see that each paragraph or group of paragraphs develops a different point.

Elsewhere we have talked about structure. Clearly the paragraphing has given this short article a very good structure.

> **Study tip**
>
> If the piece you are writing is for a leaflet, advert or pamphlet or is some other kind of publicity material, you will need to use other devices as well as, or instead of, paragraphs to divide your text into 'bite-sized' chunks that are quick and easy to follow. For example, you might use:
>
> - several short sub-headings, or
> - bullet points, like the ones being used here!

Wheelchair rugby, popularly known as 'murderball', is one of the most exciting events of the Paralympic Games. The passage which follows is an extract from an article about this sport and focuses on Kylie Grimes, the only female member of the UK Team in the 2012 Games.

Murderball: Spiked wheelchairs. Crashes galore.

By David Jones

The one-sentence opening paragraph clearly establishes the point of the article and instantly engages the reader.

The second and third paragraphs supply precise details as to the cause of Kylie's disability and its results; the final sentence of the third paragraph provides a link to the more positive picture presented by the rest of the article.

Paragraphs 4 and 5 provide a summary of Kylie's career up to the present day when she is about to compete in the 2012 Paralympic Games.

Among all the uplifting biographies in these Games, Kylie's is particularly inspirational.

Aged 18, she was a sporty student who travelled the country competing in equestrian events. Then, one night, while attending a party at a friend's home, she dived into the shallow indoor swimming pool — and her life changed in an instant. Striking her head on the bottom, she snapped her spine and was paralysed from the neck down. Even her arm movements are limited, and it seemed unlikely she would ever participate in sport again.

She at first made an attempt to sue the owner of the house where the party was held for £6 million compensation, claiming there should have been a warning sign beside the pool, but she lost the case. Nevertheless, by that time, her fortunes had undergone an astonishing transformation that no money could buy.

It came when, having attempted wheelchair racing and found it too painful to sit in the required position, her therapists at the Aspire Centre for spinal injuries in Stanmore, Middlesex, suggested she try 'murderball', in which the chair is designed differently.

She started by playing for Kent Crusaders, one of just ten teams in the UK, and showed such tactical awareness and raw courage as a defensive player that within only two years she was selected for the Paralympic squad.

Wheelchair rugby is practised in over twenty countries around the world.

▶▶

Paragraphs 6 to 8 consist of a series of comments about her daughter's strengths from Kylie's mother. This provides a wider perspective on her situation and also gives a more personal tone to the article. The final, very short paragraph effectively emphasises Kylie's determination and commitment to her sport.

The final paragraph returns to the writer's perspective and the situation in general, but also includes specific details about Kylie's appearance which leaves the reader with a strong sense of her individuality.

'Kylie was hooked on the sport as soon as she saw it,' says her mother, Karen. 'She has always been a great team-player, and from the moment she was injured she never looked back, only forward. She told me: "Mum, it's not about what I can't do — it's about what I can do."'

'At first I was nervous when I watched her, and she was sometimes thrown out of her chair. But now I don't worry because, as she says, she has already broken her neck — so there's not much worse that can happen, is there?'

'She knows she'll be hit just as hard as the men, and she wouldn't have it any other way.'

Having watched her yesterday, I have no doubt of it. Kylie is also clearly something of an exhibitionist — she has dyed her hair bright red for the Paralympics and had a Union Jack etched into a shaven section of her scalp.

From the *Daily Mail*,
5 September 2012

Tenses

Quite often students get tenses confused, swapping from present tense to past tense and back again, especially in stories. When you are writing, think carefully about the tense you are writing in – if you are writing in the present tense, then stick to it. You might want to flash back occasionally to remind your reader of something in the past, but make sure that you come back to the present after the flashback. If you are writing in the past, then stick with the past tense.

Controlling and choosing language

Your ability to control and choose how you use language is also important. You can demonstrate your ability by:

- using a variety of sentence structures to produce different effects
- using a variety of vocabulary which is appropriate for what you are writing.

In an examination, you will also need to show evidence of your ability to:

- construct an argument
- order a short story
- write persuasively.

The evidence for this will often be in the way you organise and develop your writing.

Last but not least …

Make sure your handwriting can be read easily. If only one word in three is clearly legible, the reader will gain only a partial understanding of what you are trying to say. Try to see it from the reader's point of view – the person marking your examination paper can award marks only for what he/she can read!

Study tip

If you are the sort of person whose brain works faster than your pen, then when you are writing in an examination it may be a good idea to concentrate on writing neatly. The effort involved in doing this helps to slow down your thought processes, giving you time to organise and express your ideas clearly.

Applying your reading skills: directed writing

5

There are three situations in which you may need to produce a piece of writing as part of an examination such as Cambridge IGCSE First Language English:

- as a directed writing task, in response to a reading passage and also by writing a summary
- as a composition task
- as one of the items for your coursework portfolio.

Remember, directed writing tasks also assess your reading skills and separate criteria apply for the assessment of both your reading and writing skills.

The Cambridge IGCSE First Language English Syllabus states that to fulfil the requirements for reading, you should be able to:

- demonstrate understanding of explicit meanings
- demonstrate understanding of implicit meanings and attitudes
- analyse, evaluate and develop facts, ideas and opinions
- demonstrate understanding of how writers achieve effects
- select for specific purposes.

The syllabus states that to fulfil the requirements for writing you should be able to:

- articulate, experience and express what is thought, felt and imagined
- sequence facts, ideas and opinions
- use a range of appropriate vocabulary
- use register appropriate to audience and context
- make use of spelling, punctuation and grammar.

Chapter 3 concentrates on the skills you need for successful summary writing, and Chapters 6 and 7 give advice about composition and coursework items. In this chapter, we shall look at some specific forms of 'directed writing'; the exercises and examples cover the requirements for the types of tasks you may be asked to produce in Papers 1, 2 and 3. 'Directed writing' means that you are given a clear framework for your writing. You will be given some material to read and the writing task will be very closely linked to this. So, for instance, you might be given some information to read and asked to write a letter which draws on the material you have read. This could be a letter of complaint to a company or a letter to a newspaper or magazine.

Letters are only one of a number of possible writing frameworks. We shall look at all the following possibilities in this chapter:

- a speech
- a dialogue or conversation
- a letter
- a report
- a persuasive article
- a continuation of a story
- a leaflet.

● Writing a speech

When you are writing a speech, whether it is for directed writing or for coursework, there are two very important things to remember.

1 A speech is a means of communicating with an audience – possibly quite a large audience – and you want to be sure that they all understand what you are saying. To help with this, think of more than one way of making the same point and build these into your speech. This is a key feature of a successful speech – listen out for it next time you hear someone speaking to an audience.

2 Whatever you are talking about in a speech, you want to make sure that your audience is agreeing with you as you go along. **Rhetorical questions** – questions that have an obvious, expected answer that supports the point you want to make – can help to get the audience 'on your side'. For example: 'Do we really want to see a rise in crime in our village?' or 'Is it right that children should have to work in these conditions?'

In a directed writing question, the instructions for your speech will indicate who your audience is. Think carefully about who you are addressing. For example, if you are asked to write a speech for a young audience, you will be free to use informal language which might not be appropriate for an adult audience.

Example of a speech-writing question

Read again the passage in Chapter 4, pages 57–59, 'School uniforms: turning our kids into soulless conformists' by Suzanne Moore. Then complete the following task.

> Imagine that you are taking part in an inter-school debating competition on the motion *School uniform is an out-dated concept; it should be abolished*. You are opposing the motion and, as main speaker, are replying to a speech made by Suzanne Moore. Write what you would say. Remember that your aim is to persuade your audience that wearing school uniform is a good idea.
> You should base your ideas on what you have read in the passage.

This task poses several problems.

● You are being put in a specific situation and what you write should show some understanding both of the situation and the role you have to play in it.
● You are asked to write the words of a *speech* which is intended to *persuade* your audience. You must, therefore, make what you write sound like a speech, while ensuring that you write in acceptable Standard English (see page 67). You must also concentrate on sounding persuasive.
● You must show that you have understood the ideas and content of the original passage and reply effectively to them.
● As well as keeping the main ideas of the passage in mind, you are also expected to add relevant and appropriate ideas of your own in order to present a positive argument opposing the motion.

Careful thought and planning are necessary. You must keep the task clearly focused in your mind at all times. Try to do this as you read the passage.

Writing your response

Now practise writing the words of your speech against the motion. In order to help you with this, we have provided an opening for your speech, and some ideas and advice that will help you to construct your argument in favour of wearing uniform.

'Fellow students, I would like to oppose the motion that School uniform is an out-dated concept and should be abolished. You have listened to the arguments of my opponent who has wittily and articulately presented her reasons for suggesting that school uniforms should be abolished. However, there is a lot more to consider in this matter than the points you have listened to, however skilfully they may have been made. For example, let us consider ...'

Now continue your speech from this point, focusing on the following two key aspects. First, rebut some or all of the arguments made in favour of abolishing uniform; it is important to do this because, in a directed writing task, you must show that you have understood the key points of the original passage. Second, structure your argument in such a way that you present ideas of your own in favour of uniform. You should aim to produce a forceful and memorable concluding statement.

Remember that you are writing the words of a speech. It is important to try to create a convincing oral register. This does not mean writing in an excessively colloquial way (you will be assessed on your ability to use Standard English), but you can achieve the desired effect by directly addressing your audience at different points in the speech. For example, by using direct, rhetorical questions ('How many of you save time every morning by not worrying about what to wear as you have your school uniform ready to put on?') or simply by addressing the audience ('This is a point to think seriously about, ladies and gentlemen ...').

Here are some points that you might like to include in your speech (in no particular order):

- School uniform avoids the pressure of deciding what to wear each morning and students take less time to get ready.
- Overall, uniforms are a cheaper alternative to wearing your own choice of clothes.
- Uniforms help students to identify with the school that they are part of and so create a better school spirit and a more studious environment.
- Wearing uniform helps to reduce bullying in schools as students are not judged by the designer logos on their clothes.
- Uniforms can be reused and recycled.
- Identification of intruders is made easier in a school where students are wearing the same uniform.

Exercise

This exercise can help you to practise writing a speech. Try to complete the following task based on the passages 'Protecting children from pool accidents' on pages 76–77 and 'Safe as Houses?' on pages 78–79. Again, the question identifies your audience – a group of ten-year-olds. Take this into account as you plan your talk.

There has been an increase in accidents involving young children at home.
Your teacher has given you a speaking assignment. It is to talk to a small class of ten-year-olds on the subject of keeping younger brothers and sisters safe at home. The talk is sub-titled 'How you can help'. She has given you the passages 'Protecting children from pool accidents' and 'Safe as Houses?' to start you off.
Write what you would say.

- You do not have to use all the material and you must not copy sentences from the passages.
- You might wish to include questions and comments from your ten-year-old audience.

Protecting children from pool accidents

A child's risk of drowning is much greater than most people realise, especially in residential pools.

Pools are great fun, terrific for cooling down on a hot day and for getting aerobic exercise. But they are also a responsibility. As residential pools have proliferated, so, unfortunately, has the opportunity for tragedy.

While in recent years there has been a decline in drownings among teenage boys in the United States, most of whom succumb in natural bodies of water, there has been no comparable drop in drowning deaths among young children, most of whom succumb in pools – usually the family's pool.

A child's risk of drowning is much greater than most people realise.

Children under the age of five are 14 times as likely to die in a pool as in a motor vehicle. Of those who survive near-drownings, many are permanently brain damaged.

Yet, while the vast majority of parents take care to secure their young children in car seats, far fewer take comparable precautions around pools.

Instead of adopting proven safety measures to prevent pool accidents, too many parents, grandparents and others who have residential pools rely on things like admonitions about not going near the pool alone, the false security of swimming lessons and flotation devices for toddlers, and their sincere but often misguided belief that they will watch closely and constantly when a child is in or near the pool.

A study revealed telling circumstances surrounding the pool-related deaths of young children. Two-thirds occurred in the family pool and one-third in pools owned by friends or relatives.

Nearly half the children were last seen in the house and nearly a quarter were last seen in the yard or on the porch or patio; no one knew the youngsters had gone near the pool.

Only about one-third of the children were in or around the pool just before drowning. Finally, more than three-fourths of the children had been seen five minutes or less before being missed and subsequently found in the pool.

The lessons to be learned from these statistics include the facts that drowning accidents happen very quickly, in familiar surroundings and during very short lapses in supervision.

There are no cries for help to alert caretakers that a small child is in trouble in the water. The only effective protection is to ensure that children cannot get near a pool without being accompanied by a responsible and trained caretaker whose attention is not distracted by phone calls, door bells, reading matter or the care of other children who are not in the pool.

Adopting proven safety measures is a better alternative to the false security of swimming lessons and flotation devices.

While many communities have safety regulations governing residential pools, it is the pool owner's responsibility to follow them. Regardless of local laws, to minimise the risk of pool accidents every owner should adopt these minimal safety standards:

- Fence it in. A fence or comparable barrier completely surrounding the pool is the best preventive, reducing the risk of pool drownings by about 70 per cent, an Australian study showed. It is just as important to fence in an above-ground pool as an in-ground pool, since a small child can easily climb the ladder and fall into the water.
- Cover it.
- Remain vigilant. Children in or near pools must be watched constantly by a responsible and well-informed caretaker. A moment's lapse can spell disaster. Never assume that a child who has taken swimming lessons or is using a flotation device can safely be left unattended, even just to answer the door. For added security when the caretaker is not nearby in the water, children who are not good swimmers could wear properly fitted flotation vests, which keep their heads above water.
- Prepare for emergencies. In addition to the standard ladders or steps to help people climb out of pools, there should be a circular buoy on a rope, a long-handled hook and a rescue ladder at the poolside. A poolside telephone with emergency phone numbers posted next to it is both a convenience and a critical safety feature. Anyone in charge of children playing in or near water should be trained in cardiopulmonary resuscitation and be prepared to use it the moment a child is pulled from the water. Waiting for emergency personnel to arrive can doom a nearly-drowned child.
- Observe other safety measures. Keep toys like tricycles and balls away from pools. Do not permit horseplay in the water. Children should not be allowed to dunk each other, push each other into the water or yell in jest for help. Mark the pool's deep end and, preferably, use a floating pool rope to denote where the water would be above the children's chins. Never permit diving at the shallow end or from the sides of the pool or into an above-ground pool.

From the New Straits Times, 5 July 1994

Safe as Houses?

Every year many children aged five and under are killed because of accidents in the home, and large numbers need hospital treatment. How can you make your child, grandchild or any young visitor safer in your home?

In the kitchen

The main types of injuries in the kitchen are burns and scalds, often caused by children pulling kettles full of boiling water over themselves or tipping up pans on the cooker. Other hazards include cups and teapots full of hot drinks, hot oven doors, and hot irons. Children can also be at risk from slippery kitchen floors and from household chemicals.

In the bathroom

Children can be scalded by bath water which is too hot, and they can also drown in the bath – even in only a few inches of water. Some children often like to investigate toilets, which can be unhygienic or even unsafe if some cleaning products have been used.

Slamming doors

When children are playing together it's very easy for hands or fingers to get caught in doors. Few of these injuries are serious but they're all very painful.

Falls down stairs

The under-twos are most at risk on the stairs because they try to crawl or walk up or down them before they're really ready to. Additional risks are caused by toys or other objects left on the stairs, loose carpet or poor lighting.

Falls from windows

As soon as a child is mobile, low windows, or windows with climbable objects in front of them, become a major hazard, especially on upper floors.

Fires and matches

Fire is the most common cause of accidental death in the home for children. Around half these deaths are thought to be due to children playing with matches.

Medicines and chemicals

Some houses may contain a selection of medicines and household chemicals which can be very dangerous if swallowed by small children.

Near the house

Children are also at risk near the house – particularly if they're unsupervised. Keep garages and sheds containing tools locked and take the same care with chemicals as you would in the house.

Additional exercises

1 Read carefully the passage 'A Whale of a Time in Oz!' (Chapter 1, pages 5–6).
You were on the same trip as Helen Highwater and believe strongly that we should do all we can to help conserve whales. Write the words of a speech that you would give to your year group at school in which you try to persuade them to agree with your view.
You should base what you say on the passage but you must not copy sentences from it.

2 Here are the notes of two speakers taking part in a class debate on the subject
'The car: a blessing or a curse?'

Joseph:

- Every home can have one.
- Cars are convenient and allow individual freedom to go where you like.
- You are not dependent on public transport.
- Driving is an enjoyable experience.
- They are extremely useful in emergencies.

Sunita:

- Cars emit fumes which pollute the atmosphere.
- There are too many cars on the road; it's no fun sitting in traffic jams.
- Cars are very expensive to run.
- They make people lazy; no one walks any more.
- They are dangerous, especially when driven irresponsibly.

Imagine you are either Joseph or Sunita and write the words of the speech you would give. You should use some of the ideas given above, but may also add some of your own. Remember, you might want to use some of the ideas of your opposing speaker so that you can disagree with them!

Writing a dialogue or conversation

If you are asked to write a dialogue or conversation, you are likely to be given a clear indication of how to set it out. You will almost certainly be instructed to set it out as a **playscript** with the names of the speakers on the left-hand side of the page and the words they speak on the right. If you want to give a 'direction' about how the person speaks, put it very briefly in brackets after his/her name.

James *(brightly)* It will be all right on the night.
Esmerelda *(discouragingly)* You always say that.

Example of a script-writing question

In the following question, you would be expected to take your information from the main article, the accompanying diagrams and, perhaps, the captions which relate to the diagrams (see page 81). You would also be expected to use some ideas of your own.

Once again, you are required to put yourself into a role and to write your answer as speech. However, the register (language and tone) you use for a conversation should be considerably different from that used for the formal speech we looked at on pages 74–75. It is also important that you select points from the material which would be suitable for each of the speakers in the conversation.

Imagine that you are working in a research laboratory investigating the harmful effects of noise. You have some neighbours who are worried that their children enjoy playing music very loudly. They come to you for advice.
Write a script of your conversation. Write between 25–35 lines.

Noise

Noise is a form of pollution which can be merely irritating, or cause physical or emotional damage. For some people, the sound of music played very loudly is annoying, while others revel in it. Similarly, it may be enjoyable for some to drive a motor bike, while other people find the noise anti-social.

Long-term exposure to loud noise can bring about stress which has physical signs such as an increase in oxygen consumption and heart rate, possibly leading to effects on the heart and circulation. Tiredness, irritability and sleep disturbances may also occur.

The physical effects of noise on the ears can be serious. Prolonged, loud noise causes physical discomfort; it actually 'hurts the ears'. And if it is too loud or goes on for too long, it, at first, causes temporary hearing loss, then deafness, due to permanent damage to the delicate mechanism of the inner ear. Rock musicians performing in front of very powerful speakers frequently have permanent hearing damage.

Excessive noise can have a serious effect on health, and is associated with stress and anxiety. Very loud noise causes physical damage to the delicate structures in the ear and may result in deafness.

140 — DANGER TO UNPROTECTED EAR
130 — PAIN THRESHOLD
120
110
100
90
80
70
60
50
40
30
20
10
0

HEARING THRESHOLD

TYPICAL NOISE LEVELS DECIBELS

Don't underestimate the harmful effects of noise. It is the form of pollution which has the most immediate effect on people. It can cause severe stress.

If used at too high a volume, MP3 players can cause severe hearing loss. Although the speakers are so tiny that they can fit inside the ear, the sound they produce is directed straight down the ear canal and can cause damage if the volume is turned up too high.

From *The Environment and Health*, by Brian Ward, Franklin Watts, and *Wake Up to What You Can Do for the Environment*, DETR, 1989

Key
Spelling/
punctuation errors

The stage directions are not directly relevant to the answer.

Although the opening speeches may be useful as scene-setting, they do not really contribute much to the answer as a whole.

Once the writer starts to deal with the relevant points about noise it becomes clear that he/she has understood the text and selected important points from it sensibly.

The writer's expression reveals some limitations; the material is, in places, still very close to its original leaflet format ('Tiredness, irritability and lack of sleep can occur.') and there is an overall sameness about the sentence structures. This does not provide a convincing speech register.

One of the most positive features of this answer is the way in which it manipulates the material for its own purposes. For example, the writer takes the opportunity to mention an iPod in order to include a further range of points.

Example of a student's response

(There is a knock at the door Mark gets up from his chair placing some paper work on the table. On answering the door he finds it is Jason and Carole from next door, a middle age couple with conserned looks on their faces.)

Mark (opening the door)	Hello again, how are you both?
Jason	Very well thanks, and you?
Mark (opening the door a little wider)	Work, work, work, that's all it seems to be these days. Would you like to come in?
Carole	We don't really want to bother you, if you are busy. We can come back another time. We have just got a couple of question to ask you, a bit silly really. (looking slightly embarrassed and going red)
Mark	No, come in what's on your mind

(Jason and Carole come into the hall and hold each others hand)

Jason	I remembered from the last time we spoke that you were investigating the harmful effects of noise. We just wanted some advise that's all. (looking at Carole)
Mark	I will see what I can do for you. Whats the problem.
Jason	It's the children really, they play their music far to loud and we are worried about the effects. Its driving us crazy.
Mark	Well long term exposure to noise can bring about stress, which we have found can bring about physical signs. Tiredness, irritability and lack of sleep can occur. Are they showing any of these signs?
Carole (looking at Jason)	No not that I'm awair of.
Mark	How loud do they play it?
Jason	Much louder than they need to, anyone would think they are deaf.
Mark	Physical effects on the ear are serious to. If it goes on to loud for to long, it can cause tempory hearing loss and then deafness due to perminant damage to the inner ear.
Carole	That's it, no more loud music. We will get them an iPod.
Mark	I'm afraid thats the worst thing to do, they can cause servere hearing loss, the sound goes direclty into the ear canal and causes damage. The best thing is to get them to turn in right down, to a level where everyone is happy. Noise is a polution, which can cause everyone damage.
Jason	Well thanks for that. We know what to do now, no more loud music, it was driving us mad any way.

(With a smile on their faces they turned and left.)

There are basic errors of spelling ('awair', 'tempory').

This writer has a good understanding of the task and writes a convincing conversation. However, there is some unnecessary padding and some lack of development of ideas. It is likely that this answer would achieve a top **grade C** / low **grade B** but no higher because of the weaknesses mentioned.

Exercise 1

This exercise, and the ones that follow, can help you to practise writing conversations and writing in a script format.

The following article was printed in the *New Straits Times*.
Imagine you are Mohamad Muzri Mat Sari and you are talking with a group of your friends about the day you fell off the pipe and broke your arm.
Write a page to a page and a half of the dialogue.

Dangerous balancing act to get to and return from school

By C. Navaratnam

STUDENTS living in Kampung Pasir and Taman Datuk Mansor off Jalan Rasah, Seremban, do a balancing act – one which could prove fatal – on their way to school daily.

They have become adept at carrying their bags while balancing themselves to cross a 50-metre pipe about 5 m over the Sungai Linggi.

The alternative is to walk two kilometres to school.

Some 60 students of Sekolah Menengah Jalan Loop are forced to use the pipe daily as this is the only way of crossing the river.

On rainy days, when they have to hold an umbrella and balance their bag at the same time, students do a risky 'horse ride' on the pipe which is embarrassing for the girls.

To date, a housewife has died after falling into the river. A

student has broken an arm in a similar accident.

Residents have made several appeals to State Assemblymen and Members of Parliament for a bridge across the river.

Now, they can only pray that their children make it safely across the river every time they go to and return from school.

'Yes, promises were made several times especially before the elections but nothing has been done until today. We are really disappointed,' said K. Pannir Selvam, 37, whose son uses the pipe daily.

'I think the authorities will only act when a child falls into the river. I am praying that my son will return home safely from school daily.'

Housewife Tang Chow Har, 40, recalled the day when her best friend fell while crossing the

river about 15 years ago. Her body was later found 2 km away.

'Her death was a big blow to me,' she said.

Tang said she is prepared to collect funds if the authorities are willing to build a bridge across the river.

'A bridge is essential to us as it will only take us about five minutes to reach the main road by crossing the river. If we have to use the other route, it will take us about 25 minutes,' added Tang.

Fourth-former Nur Balkiesh Sulaiman said she had no choice but to use the pipe to get to school.

'On rainy days, when it's dangerous to walk across, we have to "horse ride" the pipe to get to the other end. It is very embarrassing for us,' she said.

'We have to also bear the heat when we return tired and hungry after school. We are unable to hold an umbrella in one hand

and the books in the other while crossing,' said 15-year-old Intan Razuna Mohamad Iqbal.

Fourth-former Mohamad Muzri Mat Sari, 16, recalled the day when he fell off the pipe and broke his arm.

'It was in the morning and while I was half way along the pipeline, I slipped and fell. Thank God I did not fall into the river and I am lucky to be alive,' Mohamad Muzri said.

Several pupils admitted that it was a hazard to cross along the pipeline but preferred doing so instead of walking more than two kilometres to reach the school.

'Of course, my parents would like me to go by bus or use the other route but it is too far. My friends and I are extra cautious while crossing on the pipe,' said Form Two pupil P. Sivaraman.

'We not only have to use the pipe in the morning but also in the afternoon when we go for extramural activities.'

'We always make it a point to return before dusk,' added Sivaraman.

From the *New Straits Times*, 8 July 1994

Exercise 2

This passage is adapted from *Les Misérables*, a novel written in the nineteenth century by Victor Hugo. Cosette's mother is paying the Thénardiers to look after her but they treat her like a slave. Read carefully the passage and then complete the task which follows.

Cosette existed between the two of them, subject to pressure from either side like a creature that is at once ground between mill-stones and torn apart by pincers. Each had his own way of treating her. The blows she received came from the woman; the fact that she went barefoot in winter was due to the man. She ran upstairs and down, washed, swept, scrubbed and polished, drudged and gasped for breath, carried heavy burdens and performed arduous tasks, small though she was. There was no mercy to be expected from either mistress or master. The inn was a trap in which she was caught and held, her state of servitude the very pattern of oppression, herself the fly trembling and powerless in a spider's web.

The child endured and said nothing; but what goes on in the souls of those helpless creatures, newly arrived from God, when they find themselves thus flung naked into the world of men?

Four new travellers had arrived and Cosette was a prey to gloomy misgivings. Although she was only eight, her life had been so hard that she viewed the world already with an old woman's eyes. Her face was bruised by a blow from Mme Thénardier, which caused that lady to remark, 'She looks a sight with that black eye.'

She was thinking as she sat under the table that the night was very dark, and that the jugs and pitchers in the bedrooms of the new arrivals had had to be filled, so that there was no more water in the house. There was some reassurance in the fact that not much water was drunk in the tavern. They had no lack of thirsty customers, but it was a thirst calling for wine, not water.

Nevertheless she was given cause to tremble. Mme Thénardier lifted the lid of a cooking pot bubbling on the stove, then seized a glass and went over to the water-butt, while the little girl watched her in alarm. Only a thin trickle came when she turned the tap, half-filling the glass, and she exclaimed, 'Bother! We're out of water.'

There was a moment of silence while Cosette held her breath.

'Don't worry,' said Thénardier, looking at the half-filled glass. 'That'll be enough.'

Cosette went on with her work, but her heart was thumping. She counted the minutes as they dragged by, praying for it to be tomorrow morning. Every now and then a customer would put his head outside and say, 'It's black as pitch. You'd need to be a cat to get about without a lantern on a night like this,' and she would tremble afresh.

Then a traveller who was stopping in the house came into the general room and said angrily:

'My horse hasn't been watered.'

'Indeed it has,' said Mme Thénardier.

'I tell you it hasn't, mistress,' the man said.

Cosette scrambled out from under the table.

'But he has, monsieur. I took him water myself, a whole bucketful, and I talked to him.'

This was not true. Cosette was lying.

'No higher than my knee and lies like a trooper!' the traveller cried. 'I tell you he hasn't, my girl. I know it for sure. When he's thirsty he snorts in a particular way.'

Cosette stuck to her guns, speaking in a voice so stifled with terror as to be scarcely audible.

'All the same, he has.'

'Look,' said the man angrily, 'there's not much in watering a horse, is there? Why not just do it?'

Cosette dived back under the table.

'Well, that's right,' said Mme Thénardier. 'If the horse hasn't been watered it ought to be. Where's the girl got to now?' She peered under the table and saw her crouched at the far end, almost under the drinkers' feet. 'Come out of there, you!'

Cosette crept out again.

'Now, Miss good-for-nothing, go and water that horse.'

'But, Madame,' said Cosette faintly, 'there's no water left.'

Mme Thénardier's answer was to fling open the street door.

'Then go and get some,' she said.

Disconsolately Cosette fetched an empty bucket from a corner of the hearth. It was larger than herself, large enough for her to have sat in it. Mme Thénardier turned back to her stove and dipping in a wooden spoon tasted the contents of the pot.

'Plenty of water in the spring,' she muttered. 'No trouble at all. I think this could have done without the onions.'

She went over to a drawer in which she kept small change and other oddments.

'Here, Miss Toad,' she said. 'Here's a fifteen-sou piece. While you're about it you can get a large loaf at the baker's.'

Cosette took the coin without a word and put it carefully in the pocket of her apron. Then, with the bucket in her hand, she stood hesitating in the doorway, as though hoping someone would rescue her.

'Get a move on,' cried Mme Thénardier.

Cosette went out and the door closed behind her.

From Les Misérables by Victor Hugo

> Imagine that you are a friend of Cosette's mother and you meet Cosette in the street immediately following the events described in the passage above. Write the conversation that you have with her.

Exercise 3

Read carefully the passage 'Thank God … it's a miracle' (Chapter 1, pages 8–9) and then complete the following task.

> Imagine you are a newspaper reporter interviewing Tony Bullimore about his experience. Write the text of your conversation.

Exercise 4

Read carefully the article 'School uniforms: turning our kids into soulless conformists' (Chapter 4, pages 57–59) and then complete the following task.

> You are the host of a television talk show and your guests are the writer Suzanne Moore and a headteacher of a successful school with a strict uniform policy. Write the words of a discussion that develops between you and your two guests.

Exercise 5

Read carefully the passage on wheelchair rugby (Chapter 3, pages 71–72) and then complete the following task.

> You are the host of a television talk show and your guests are Kylie Grimes and her mother.
> You talk to Kylie about what she has achieved so far and how she would like her career to develop.
> You also ask her mother for her thoughts about her daughter and the dangerous sport in which she takes part. Write the words of the discussion which develops between you and your two guests.

● Writing a letter

You may be asked to read some information and write a letter in response. The following are just three examples of the type of letter you might be asked to write:

- a letter of complaint or enquiry to a company
- a letter to a magazine or newspaper, commenting on the material and giving your reaction
- a letter explaining or apologising for a problem.

As with any piece of writing, remember to think about the **audience** and the **purpose**.

1 **Who are you writing to?** This will help you to decide how formal your letter needs to be. If it is a letter to a friend, for instance, it can be in a chatty style and you can use some informal, colloquial language. For example, instead of 'I feel I must express my views on …' it would be more appropriate to say 'I must tell you what I thought about …'.

2 **What are you writing for?** Is it to complain, to make a request, to apologise, or to defend or attack a particular point of view? The answer to this question will have an effect on how you write. For example, if it is a letter to a company then your points must be clearly ordered and written in a systematic, logical way.

One important point: even if your letter is making a complaint about a situation or attacking someone else's opinion, it should never be abusive or rude.

How should your letter be set out?

Although the layout of a letter may not be as important as the content, you should follow certain guidelines. Study the layouts for a personal letter and a formal letter below and on the next page, and use them appropriately. You must set your letter out neatly; there is never any excuse for an untidy-looking letter.

A personal letter to a friend or relative

7 Hillside Close
Anytown
Blankshire
AB1 2YZ

1 September 2013

Put your address at the top right-hand corner, with the date underneath it.

Dear Claire

_____

_____

_____

_____

_____

_____

_____

_____

_____

_____

_____

_____

Use an informal ending.

With love from

A formal letter

Put your address at the top right-hand corner.

7 Hillside Close
Anytown
Blankshire
AB1 2YZ

Put the name and address of the person you are writing to on the left-hand side of the page.

Mr Brown
Head of Leisure Services
Blankshire Council
Council Offices
Anytown
Blankshire
AB4 6JQ

Put the date below this address.

2 September 2013

If you don't know the name of the person you are writing to, start 'Dear Sir/Madam'.

Dear Mr Brown

_____

_____

_____

_____

_____

_____

_____

_____

_____

If you used the person's name at the start of the letter, end with 'Yours sincerely'. If you started the letter 'Dear Sir/Madam', end with 'Yours faithfully'. If you know the person you are writing to quite well, you could end your letter more informally: 'With best wishes', for example.

Yours sincerely

Examples of letters

Read these two letters about a dog that got out of control.

The letter starts by getting straight to the point.

A development paragraph clearly explains exactly what happened.

The third paragraph neatly rounds off the letter with a return to the opening.

The letter started with a name, so the ending is correct.

Dear Mrs Arensky,

I would like to apologise for the unfortunate incident that I caused in your mini-market last Thursday. I have talked it over with my parents who have suggested that I write to you to explain how it happened.

I admit that it was my fault in bringing my pet mouse, Minnie, into your shop in the first place. She was in a box as I was taking her to my friend's house as she was going to look after Minnie for me while I was away on a school trip. Unfortunately, as I approached the meat counter, I bumped against one of your fixtures, dropped the box and Minnie escaped. She set off with me behind her. As she scampered around, many of the other shoppers started to panic. One lady screamed and jumped out of the way and, without looking where she was heading, fell into a pile of eggs which crashed to the floor and broke. People started to slip over, and in no time at all there was total disorder. I eventually managed to recapture Minnie who had stopped to eat some soft fruit that another customer had dropped.

Although it was really just an accident, I realise that it is my responsibility to apologise and to offer to pay for the damage. My parents have generously said they will lend me the money which I can pay back over what will probably have to be a very long period of time.

Yours sincerely,

Olga Mishkin

Dear Mrs Arensky,

My parents have made me write this letter though I don't think it's fair. You should blame the person who left the fixture sticking out into the aisle of the shop. You can't blame Minnie for escaping when I dropped her as she doesn't know any better and you can't blame me for chasing after her. And you have to admit it is a bit silly to put all those eggs there. They're just asking to be knocked over, aren't they. You see, Minnie isn't used to having a large space to run around in and I couldn't stop her from running off and did my best to stop her by shouting out to her. Anyway, half the trouble was your shoppers. They didn't look where they were going. So they bumped into each other. I thought it was funny when my my maths teacher Mr Lee got trapped against the tins of vegetables and they all collapsed on him. I mean you have to laugh, don't you.

Yours,

Olga Mishkin

No paragraphing and the content is not ordered.

The tone of the letter is all wrong – it is not apologetic but it is complaining.

The content of the letter is distorted as Olga tries to shift the blame.

Given that this is a formal letter, the ending is incorrect. It should be 'Yours sincerely'.

Exercise 1

This exercise, and the ones that follow, can help you to practise writing a letter. Read again the article on pages 83–84 with the headline 'Dangerous balancing act to get to and return from school'. Then complete the following task.

> You are one of the students who has to use the pipe daily to get to and from school.
> Write a letter to the authorities asking them to consider building a bridge across the river. Include:
>
> - reference to the facts
> - reference to the dangers, including reference to accidents that have occurred
> - your own feelings as someone who has to use the pipe on rainy days.
>
> Write between a page and a page and a half.

Exercise 2

Study the online advertisement below and on pages 91–92 and then complete the task which follows.

ADOPT A DOLPHIN NOW

And you will receive:

- **A WDC adoption pack**
- **A certificate of adoption**
- **A WDC cotton bag**
- **Free magazine subscription**
- **Dolphin updates throughout the year**

She's beautiful. She's intelligent. Don't let her die.

Every two minutes another dolphin like Kesslet suffers a slow, agonising death, accidentally trapped in fishing nets. Help end the suffering.

More than 300,000 dolphins die in fishing nets every year.

You can help save dolphins around the world by adopting a UK dolphin for just £4 a month. Adopt now.

WDC, Whale and Dolphin Conservation, is the leading global charity dedicated to the conservation and protection of whales and dolphins.

We defend these remarkable creatures against the many threats that they face through campaigns, lobbying, advising governments, conservation projects, field research and rescue.

Our vision is a world where every whale and dolphin is safe and free – including the dolphin you adopt.

Meet the dolphins

The dolphins each have their own personalities – click on the dolphin you'd like to adopt.

The dolphins of Scotland's Moray Firth are amazing but they face many threats. When you adopt a dolphin you will build a special link with an individual and help us to protect the whole population and give them a safer future.

Kesslet

Kesslet is a young mum who likes to hunt and play with her calf, Charlie. Kesslet is easy to spot because of her curved dorsal fin. She is friends with lots of the local dolphins like Rainbow and Moonlight and can be often seen travelling in groups of mums and youngsters.

Mischief

Mischief is a very friendly male dolphin who is always in a party mood! He is often seen in big groups leaping around with friends such as Rainbow and Sundance. Mischief is also a powerful hunter who can outrun even the biggest salmon. He is easily recognised by the big nick in his dorsal fin.

Sundance

Sundance was first spotted in 1990 when he was a tiny calf and now he's a big adult male bottlenose dolphin. Sundance is really sociable and he just loves to leap around with friends – especially Moonlight. We think he may be dad to Moonlight's baby.

Rainbow

Rainbow was first spotted way back in 1989 when she was just a youngster. She now has calves of her own including Raindrop who was born in 2005. She got her name because of her 'bright and colourful' character! She has a nick in the centre of her dorsal fin, which makes her easy to spot.

▶▶

Moonlight

Moonlight was first spotted in 1996 when she was very young. She now has calves of her own, including Mellow Yellow. She is easy to identify by the twin notches near the top of her dorsal fin. Moonlight loves to socialise with her best friend Rainbow. She's an amazing hunter – especially when she's in hot pursuit of lunch!

Spirit

Spirit was given her name due to her gentle and spirited nature. She has a calf called Sparkle, who was born in July 2007. She is often seen in the company of the other mums and their babies. Spirit has two very sharp nicks in her dorsal fin which make her easy to recognise.

Why adopt a dolphin?

'I can thoroughly recommend adopting a dolphin with WDC. It's a fantastic way to support their amazing work. Plus, you get to know an individual dolphin!' says Miranda Krestovinikoff, WDC Patron and BBC TV Presenter.

Oil and gas exploration and production, large marina development, pollution, fisheries and more are increasingly putting pressure on the dolphins and their home. By adopting a dolphin, you will build a special link with an individual and help us to protect the whole population. Extinction is forever – the Moray Firth dolphins cannot be replaced.

These dolphins face many threats.

When you adopt a dolphin you will be helping to fund our work protecting dolphins around the world including:

- Essential research – the more we understand about the dolphins, the better we can protect them.
- Political campaigns to ensure effective laws are in place to protect the dolphins and give them a safer future.
- Equipment such as binoculars, cameras and acoustic recorders to help with our research.

Adapted from WDC (Whale and Dolphin Conservation)

You have been asked to give a talk to parents of students in your year group at school to encourage them and their families to adopt a dolphin. Write the words of your talk.

- You should select details from the advertisement, but do not try to use everything.
- Remember that your speech should be persuasive.

Writing a report

The key to writing a successful report is to organise your facts clearly. A report concentrates primarily on information, though it may well be leading to a particular conclusion or opinion.

- Use headings to make it clear what your main points are: start with one major heading, and use others to divide your writing into short sections.
- Before you start writing, decide on the headings you want to use and make lists under these headings; this will help to ensure that in your final piece the facts are presented in an organised way.
- The sections or paragraphs of a report should be shorter than they usually are when you are writing stories or compositions. This helps the reader to assess the information quickly.
- A report is written for a particular readership. Make sure you know who the readership is before you start.

Writing a journalistic report

The key points given above about report-writing also apply to the writing of journalistic (news or magazine) reports. However, journalistic reports have a few special features.

- They usually start with a headline. Choose one which sets the tone for what comes after – are you reporting a tragic or shocking event, or a funny or surprising event, or are you giving a straightforward account of a recent political decision, for example?
- A journalistic report often contains transcripts (written records) of interviews, or extracted quotes from those, which are reported verbatim (word for word). If you choose to use this technique, you must either use speech marks correctly or turn the interview into reported speech.

Example of a news report

Look at the key features of a news report, highlighted on this article.

This type of article needs a headline.

Miracle Escape at Busy Crossing

There is an introductory paragraph which summarises the content.

At midday today, a cyclist who lost control of his bicycle narrowly missed death as he swerved round an articulated lorry and a small car. The small car subsequently hit a lamp post but fortunately no one was injured. Chaos was caused when the lorry shed part of its load.

Paragraphs are short, much shorter than in a piece of continuous writing.

The incident happened when Inderjit Singh, 32, of 46 Victory Road, found that the brakes on his bicycle had failed. 'I was riding quickly towards the junction and the traffic lights were red. It is all downhill you know. When I applied my brakes, nothing happened. I just went hurtling towards the junction.'

Articles of this type gain enormously from quotations from the people involved.

The driver of the lorry, Wing Koh, 45, of 123 Main Street, was moving away from the lights when he saw Inderjit Singh. He said that he had no chance to avoid the cyclist who managed to avoid him by executing a smart manoeuvre. Wing Koh added that as the front of his lorry swooped round, he found himself heading for a small yellow car travelling in the opposite direction.

'a write-off' says visitor

The driver of the car, Rejoice Ntuli, a visitor to our city, was only just able to avoid the cyclist. 'I braked hard,' she said, 'and my car swerved to the right, hitting a lamp post. The car is a write-off, but I think that I am all right.'

The police were called to the scene as traffic was brought to a standstill. The lorry shed part of its load of colourful mechanical toy animals, some of which were set in motion by the accident and caused bystanders much amusement.

no prosecution

An official statement from the police revealed that no one would be prosecuted as a result of the incident. Inderjit Singh thanked the police for their assistance and said that he was happy to be alive.

Extracted quotes give the reader a quick guide.

Exercise 1

This exercise, and the ones that follow, can help you to practise writing a report. Your school is planning to choose a new School Captain for the next academic year. Here are details of two of the candidates. Read each one carefully and then complete the task which follows.

Morgan

Age: 17

Joined school in Grade 7 at age of 11.

Academic progress

Disappointing progress during Grades 7–10. Frequently in trouble for minor misdemeanours. Many complaints from teachers about lapses of concentration during lessons. Attitude to study changed significantly from Grade 11 onwards. Gained good IGCSE grades in all subjects and is now studying A Levels. Plans to read Medicine at university.

Extra-curricular activities

Has always been committed to a wide range of sporting activities and has captained school teams throughout school career. Always punctual for matches and has contributed much to the school's sporting successes over the last few years.

Other interests include cycling – recently completed a 1000 km sponsored cycle ride for charity; socialising and playing online video games.

Extract from letter of application

'I feel I have a lot to offer as School Captain. As a result of my sporting successes, I am very well known in the school and am very popular with members of the teams that I captain. I don't see there being any difference between captaining a sports team and captaining a school …

I know I gave the teachers a bit of hassle in my earlier years but that's behind me now and my earlier school life means that I can empathise with the less motivated students.'

Leigh

Age: 17

Joined school in Grade 10 when family emigrated to this country.

Academic progress

Rapidly became one of the best academic students in the school. Has won prizes for being the top all-round performer in the year for the last three years. At the end of Grade 12 was awarded the prestigious Newton Prize for being the most promising young physicist in the state. Has already been accepted to read Astrophysics at Cambridge University in the UK (dependent on A Level grades).

Extra-curricular activities

Member of school chess club and competes for school in orienteering competitions. Is a leading light in the school's debating society and represents the school in the local area's Schools' Council.

Relaxes by going to the cinema and by reading science fantasy novels.

Extract from letter of application

'My experience on the local Schools' Council means that I am very aware of the main issues relating to the education of students in this region and I will ensure that the views of students of this school will be fully made known …

Joining the school only a few years ago means that I have experience of the education system in other countries and I can use this to the advantage of all.'

Imagine that you are a member of the committee of senior students and teachers in your school responsible for making a shortlist of candidates for the position of School Captain. You have been asked to consider the merits of Morgan and Leigh.

Write a report for the other members of the committee in which you explain your views on these two candidates. You may:

- prefer one candidate to the other
- decide that neither is suitable
- urge the committee to consider both of them.

You should write between a page and a page and a half.

Exercise 2

Read carefully the two articles on the Efteling Theme Park on pages 52–54 (Chapter 3) and then complete the following task.

> Write a report for a youth group to which you belong, giving reasons as to why the group should arrange an outing to the theme park.

Exercise 3

> Imagine you are Robert Ballard, the author of the following article. A salvage company has asked your advice as to whether the *Titanic* can and should be raised from the sea bed. Write a report for the company in which you give details of the condition and situation of the *Titanic* and your recommendations as to why there should or should not be an attempt made to raise it.

Our second view of the *Titanic* was breathtaking. As we glided across the bottom, out of the darkness loomed the vertical knife-edge of the bow – the great ship towered above us and suddenly it seemed to be coming right at us, about to run our little submarine down. Gently we brought the sub closer until we could see the bow more clearly. It was buried more than sixty feet in bottom mud. Both anchors still hung in place.

Rivers of rust covered the side of the ship, some of it running the full length of the exposed vertical hull plating and pouring out over the bottom sediment where it formed great ponds as much as thirty to forty feet across. The blood of the great ship lay in pools on the ocean floor. Then, as we rose in slow motion up the ghostly wall of the port bow, our running lights reflected off the still unbroken glass of the portholes in a way that made me think of eyes gleaming in the dark. In places, the rust about them formed eyelashes, sometimes tears: as though the *Titanic* were weeping over her

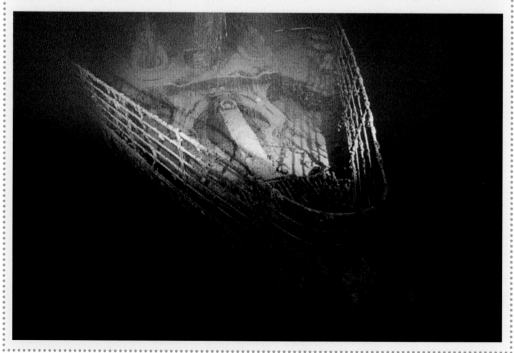

fate. Near the upper railing – still largely intact – reddish-brown stalactites of rust, the result of rust-eating bacteria, hung down as much as several feet, looking like long icicles. I subsequently dubbed them 'rusticles', a name which seems to have stuck.

These rust features turned out to be very fragile. If touched by 'Alvin' (that was the name we called our sub), or dislodged by the thrust from one of our propellers, they disappeared in a cloud of smoke. And once the foamy crust had been knocked away, the steel beneath appeared almost perfectly preserved, only slightly pitted.

Carefully I counted the portholes aft from the anchor to locate the position where the ship's name should be, but I could see nothing.

Alvin rose farther, cleared the railing forward of No. 1 hatch, and we manoeuvred in over the *Titanic's* mighty forward deck. All at once I was forcibly struck by the sheer size of everything: giant bollards, the huge links of the anchor chains, and even bigger shiny bronze-topped capstans. Until now the ship for me had been somehow ghostly, distant, incorporeal. Now it was very close, very real.

I strained to get a look at the deck's wooden planking just four feet below us. Then my heart dropped. Gone was any hope of finding much *Titanic* woodwork intact, her beauty unblemished by the years. Except for a few fragments here and there, the wood was replaced by thousands upon thousands of small, white, hollow calcareous tubes one or two inches in length – the protective home of wood-boring molluscs.

I began to wonder whether the metal sub-deck would support us when Alvin made her first landing.

From *The Discovery of the Titanic*, Robert Ballard, Orion, 1995

● Writing a persuasive article

A persuasive article must be clear and well structured. For example, you might well start with a point, develop it and then return to it in the last sentences to emphasise that it is the important point of the article.

- A certain amount of bias is likely in a persuasive article. For instance, a report on a football match written for the local newspaper of the home side might be rather different from a report written for the local newspaper of the away side. It might be different in the claims it makes about which individuals played best, who tried hardest, or what the highlights of the match were. However, if an article is too obviously biased, no one will take it seriously, so you have to **include some convincing facts, not just opinions**. The persuasiveness depends on the facts you select and how clearly you present them.
- Quotations can be used effectively in a persuasive piece, so long as you select those which support the point of view you want to put across.

Look back at the example of a persuasive piece of writing in Chapter 4 (pages 57–59). You will find that it includes some consideration of both sides of the argument and this is more convincing than a one-sided argument would have been.

Exercise 1

This exercise, and the ones that follow, can help you to practise writing a persuasive article. On pages 8–9 in Chapter 1 there is an article about a British sailor whose boat overturned, leaving him trapped. Others then had to risk their lives to save him. People have various attitudes towards this sort of incident.

> Write an article in which you try to persuade your readers that people who get into difficulties while taking part in dangerous sports or outdoor activities have only themselves to blame and other people should not risk their own lives to help them.

Exercise 2

Read carefully the following extract from a website 'Threatened Species'.
Then complete the task which follows.

Nearly one-quarter of the world's known mammal species are threatened with extinction or are already extinct according to a recent study compiled by the IUCN (World Conservation Union). This suggests that earlier estimates of the number of endangered species must have been too low.

The latest update in a series known as The Red List, the report is the most comprehensive evaluation of globally threatened animals ever compiled, and the first to assess all known mammal species.

STEMLESS GENTIAN
Gentiana acaulis

© Malcolm Scott (CC BY-NC 2.0 UK)

Until now, birds were the only group fully assessed. With 12% of all bird species facing the threat of extinction and 70% experiencing population declines, scientists had relied largely on the status of birds as an indicator of the level of threat to all terrestrial life forms.

The number of mammals on The Red List – a shocking 1219 of the 5487 known species – has spurred calls for an intensified international focus on biodiversity loss. The report also found that nearly half of all 414 primate species are at risk, much more than thought in previous estimates.

The new survey was compiled using a revised set of criteria, which the authors described as more objective than those used in previous estimates, to determine the threat of extinction. The Red List recognises three distinct categories of risk: of the mammals considered threatened, 188 species are listed as 'critically endangered', 448 as 'endangered', and 505 as 'vulnerable'. Each classification is largely determined by the rate of a species' population decline over the past 10 years, as well as the number of surviving adults and the stability of habitat.

George Rabb, ex-chair of the IUCN species survival commission which compiled the list, said that the report should serve as a 'red flag', focusing attention on the most significant factor threatening the survival of species: the destruction of habitat brought about by human population growth and economic development.

Other contributing factors, he said, include pollution, overharvesting, and the introduction of foreign species. At current rates of decline, biologists fear that many mammals with niches or habitat needs that conflict with human development may soon come to depend on the tinkering hand of wildlife management and captive breeding – unable to exist without human intervention.

From The Worldwatch Institute, www.worldwatch.org,
IUCN Red List, www.iucnredlist.org, 2008

Using the information in the extract above as a basis for your argument, write a persuasive article for a teenage magazine to encourage your readers to help save animals threatened by extinction.

● Writing a continuation of a story

Another directed writing question which you may be set is to write a continuation of a story. There are a few important points to keep in mind when tackling this type of task.

The person reading your response will **not** have a list of key points of content that they will expect you to include. *However*, they will expect you to follow certain conventions. The main ones are listed below.

- Remember that whatever you write as a continuation of a story must be relevant to the ideas in the passage you have already read. Occasionally, students try to use this type of task as an opportunity to repeat a composition they have written during their course, even though it has very little connection with the subject of the story. This approach is not advised as it is almost certain that you will be found out and be awarded very low marks. (Incidentally, this point about relevance applies equally to continuous writing.)
- Your continuation should make use of the pointers contained in the original story and lead towards a conclusion which could convincingly follow on from what you have already read. Try to ensure that the way you write about the characters in the story is consistent with what you already know about them. Read the original story carefully to make sure you pick up any hints that indicate how events are likely to develop.
- Remember to continue the story by using the same narrative conventions as the original. For example, if the original story was written in the first person ('I did', etc.) then your continuation should also be written in the first person. You should also make sure that you use the same tense as that used in the original story.
- As far as possible, you should try to write in a similar style to that of the original. Some attempt to follow the type of sentence structures, adjectives, similes and metaphors used by the author of the original will be seen as a positive feature of your writing.

Example of a continuation of a story question

Here is an example of a question requiring you to continue a story. The student's response which follows on page 102 will help to clarify some of the points we have made. (All spelling and punctuation mistakes have been corrected in order to allow you to concentrate on the content and style of the story.)

> The time when the rains didn't come for three months and the sun was a yellow furnace in the sky was known as the Great Drought in Trinidad. It happened when everyone was expecting the sky to burst open with rain to fill the dry streams and water the parched earth.
>
> But each day was the same; the sun rose early in a blue sky, and all day long the farmers lifted their eyes, wondering what had happened to Parjanya, the rain god. They rested on their hoes and forks and wrung perspiration from their clothes, seeing no hope in labour, terrified by the thought that if no rain fell soon they would lose their crops and livestock and face starvation and death.
>
> In the tiny village of Las Lomas, out in his vegetable garden, Manko licked dry lips and passed a wet sleeve over his dripping face. Somewhere in

the field a cow mooed mournfully, sniffing around for a bit of green in the cracked earth. The field was a desolation of drought. The trees were naked and barks peeled off trunks as if they were diseased. When the wind blew, it was heavy and unrelieving, as if the heat had taken all the spirit out of it. But Manko still opened his shirt and turned his chest to it when it passed.

He was a big man, grown brown and burnt from years of working on the land. His arms were bent and he had a crouching position even when he stood upright. When he laughed he showed more tobacco stain than teeth.

But Manko had not laughed for a long time. Bush fires had swept Las Lomas and left the garden plots charred and smoking. Cattle were dropping dead in the heat. There was scarcely any water in the village; the river was dry with scummy mud. But with patience one could collect a bucket of water. Boiled, with a little sugar to make it drinkable, it had to do.

Sometimes, when the children knew that someone had gone to the river for water, they hung about in the village main road waiting with bottles and calabash shells, and they fell upon the water-carrier as soon as he hove in sight.

'Boil the water first before drinking!' was the warning cry. But even so two children were dead and many more were on the sick list, their parents too poor to seek medical aid in the city twenty miles away.

Manko sat in the shade of a mango tree and tried to look on the bright side of things. Such a dry season meant that the land would be good for corn seeds when the rains came. He and his wife Rannie had been working hard and saving money with the hope of sending Sunny, their son, to college in the city.

Rannie told Manko: 'We poor, and we ain't have no education, but is all right, we go get old soon and dead, and what we have to think about is the boy. We must let him have plenty learning and come a big man in Trinidad.'

And Manko, proud of his son, used to boast in the evening, when the villagers got together to talk and smoke, that one day Sunny would be a lawyer or a doctor.

But optimism was difficult now. His livestock was dying out, and the market was glutted with yams. He had a great pile in the yard which he could not sell. Manko took a look at his plot of land and shook his head. There was no sense in working any more today. He took his cutlass and hoe and calabash shell which had a string so he could hold it dangling. He shook it, and realised with burning in his throat that it was empty, though he had left a few mouthfuls in it. He was a fool; he should have known that the heat would dry it up if he took it out in the garden with him. He licked his lips and, shouldering the tools, walked slowly down the winding path which led to his hut.

From *A Drink of Water* by Samuel Selvon

'After another month the rains came.' Continue the story until the moment the rainclouds appear.

- Make Manko the main character.
- Use what you have learned about Manko, his family and life in the village.
- Write between a page and a page and a half.

Example of a student's response

Time passed. Every morning Manko awoke and looked hopefully at the sky. The burning sun looked back at him, mockingly.

The pile of yams became smaller. Rannie, Sunny and Manko had eaten them and drunk the boiled dirty water from the river. This was all they had to eat for days.

Rannie had grown weak and become ill. Manko was worried: she was feverish but he had no spare water with which he could bathe her burning forehead.

Manko sat by Rannie's side holding her hand as she lay on the floor of the hut. He felt that his great strength too was fading away. He had not laughed now for many months. He had watched his animals slowly dying from starvation and lack of water to drink. There were very few of them remaining by now. If the rains were to come soon there might be just enough to allow him to rebuild his stock. If the rains did not come he dared not think what would happen. The water in the river was by now no more than a tiny trickle.

Only Sunny kept their spirits alive. The boy lived up to his name. On this day he had gone to the river to find what water he could. Manko talked quietly to Rannie. Soon the rain would come, he told her. All would be well: Sunny would be able to go to college.

'Father, Father, come quickly.'

He heard Sunny shouting outside the hut and rushed out to see what was upsetting him. Rannie struggled to her feet and walked slowly to the door.

'Father, look … look!'

Manko was worried. Had his son hurt himself? He was standing outside the hut pointing at … nothing.

'What is it, Sunny? My old eyes are weak. What can you see?'

'Father, look at the sun.'

Manko screwed up his eyes and peered at the sun. Could it be true? Yes, it was. Slowly, surely, a black cloud was covering the burning, golden ball. The sky had turned from blue to deep grey. Great, heavy clouds were approaching.

'Father, can you see now? The clouds … they are bringing rain.'

Rannie had joined them now. Manko embraced his wife and his son. The rains were coming. Within minutes, great, heavy drops of water were soaking them to the skin. The ground had turned to mud and already green shoots were beginning to appear.

Manko stood soaked and happy. Now he could plant his corn seeds. Maybe Sunny would be an important man after all.

Teacher's comment: The writer of this continuation has made a positive attempt to follow the style and content of the original story and to use the suggestions given in the wording of the question. The writer has wisely not attempted to produce too ambitious a story but has concentrated on a single event. Remember that you are working under time restrictions.

The continuation makes some attempt to imitate the sentence structures of the original and shows an awareness of the type of descriptive techniques it uses, in particular, through the ways in which the sun is repeatedly referred to and described. The writer also tries hard to include details from the original story. For example, he/she brings in references to the dying cattle, the corn seeds and the description of Manko as a tall man who used to laugh a lot. The continuation also shows that the writer has understood the relationship between Manko and Rannie and, in particular, their hopes for Sunny.

The impression given by this piece of writing to a teacher reading it would be a positive one. It may not be the continuation of the story which the author of the original had in mind, but what has been written is consistent with what has gone before and is perfectly credible. It is worth a **grade** A–B for its content and its attempt to follow the style of the original. A continuation which concluded with a much less happy ending would also have been perfectly acceptable, as long as it showed similar merits of structure, style and content.

Exercise

This exercise can help you to practise writing a continuation of a story. Read carefully the story 'The Gold-Legged Frog' and then complete the task which follows.

THE GOLD-LEGGED FROG

by Khamsing Srinawk

The sun blazed as if determined to crisp every living thing in the broad fields. Now and again the tall, straight, isolated *sabang* and *payom* trees let go some of their dirty yellow leaves. He sank exhausted against a tree trunk with his dark blue shirt wet with sweat. The expanse round him expressed total dryness. He stared at the tufts of dull grass and bits of straw spun in a column to the sky. The brown earth sucked up into the air cast a dark pall over everything. A whirlwind. He recalled the old people had told him this was the portent of drought, want, disaster and death, and he was afraid. He was now anxious to get home; he could see the tips of the bamboo thickets surrounding the house far ahead looking like blades of grass. But he hesitated. A moment before reaching the shade of the tree he felt his ears buzz and his eyes blur and knew it meant giddiness and sunstroke. He looked at the soles of his feet blistered from the burning sandy ground and became indescribably angry – angry with the weather capable of such endless torture. In the morning the cold had pierced his bones, but now it was so hot he felt his head would break into bits and pieces. As he remembered the biting cold of the morning, he thought again of his little son.

●　　●　　●　　●

That same morning he and two of his small children went out into the dry paddy fields near the house to look for frogs for the morning meal. The air was so chilly the two children on either side of him shivered as they stopped to look for frogs hiding in the cracks of the parched earth. Each time they saw two bright eyes in a deep crack, they would shout, 'Pa, here's another one. Pa, this crack has two. Gold-legged ones! Hurry, Pa.'

He dashed from place to place as the voices called him, prying up the dry clods with his hoe. He caught some of the frogs immediately, but a few

▶▶

jumped away as soon as he began digging. It was the children's job to chase and pounce on them. Many got away. Some jumped into different fissures obliging him to prise up a new cake of earth. If his luck was good, besides the frog, he would find a land snail or razor clam buried waiting for the rains. He would take these as well.

The air was warming and already he had enough frogs to eat with the morning rice. The sound of drumming, the village chief's call for a meeting, sounded faintly from the village. Vague anger again spilled over as his thoughts returned to that moment. If only he had gone home then the poor child would be all right now. It was really the last crack. As soon as he poked it, the ground broke apart. A fully grown gold-legged frog as big as a thumb leaped past the bigger child. The younger raced after it for about twelve yards when it dodged into the deep hoofprint of a water buffalo. The child groped after it. And then he was shocked almost senseless by the trembling cry of his boy, 'Pa, a snake, a snake bit my hand.'

A cobra spread its hood, hissing. When finally able to act, the father with all his strength brought the handle of his hoe three times down on the back of the serpent leaving its tail twitching. He carried his child and the basket of frogs home without forgetting to tell the other to drag the snake along as well.

On the way back his son cried softly and moaned, beating his chest with his fists and complaining he could not breathe. At home, the father summoned all the faith-healers and herbalists whose names he could think of and the turmoil began.

'Chop up a frog, roast it, and put it on the wound,' a neighbour called out.

When another shouted, 'Give him the toasted liver of the snake to eat,' he hurriedly slit open the snake to look for the liver while his wife sat by crying. The later it got, the bigger the crowd. On hearing the news, all the neighbours attending the village chief's meeting joined the others. One of them told him he had to go to the District Office in town that day because the village chief told them it was the day the government was going to hand out money to those with five or more children, and he was one who had just five. It was a new shock.

'Can't you see my boy's gasping out his life? How can I go?'

'What difference will it make? You've called in a lot of doctors, all of them expert.'

'Go, you fool. It's two hundred baht they're giving. You've never had that much in your life-time. Two hundred!'

'Leave this for a bit,' another added. 'If the boy dies, you'll be out, that's all.'

'I won't go,' he yelled. 'My child can't breathe and you tell me to go. Why can't they give it out some other day? It's true I've never had two hundred baht since I was born, but I'm not going. I'm not going.'

'Jail,' another interjected. 'If you don't go, you simply go to jail. Whoever disobeyed the authorities? If they decide to give, you have to take. If not, jail.'

The word 'jail' repeated like that affected him, but still, he resisted.

'Whatever it is, I said I'm not going. I don't want it. How can I leave him when he's dying?' He raised his voice. 'I'm not going.'

'You go. Don't go against the government. We're subjects.' He turned to find the village chief standing grimly at his side. His voice dried up immediately.

'If I don't go, will it really be jail?' he asked.

'For sure,' the village chief replied sternly. 'Maybe for life.'

That was all there was to it. Dazed, he asked the faith-healers and neighbours to take care of his son and left the house.

From *The Politician and other stories*, by Khamsing Srinawk, Oxford University Press, 1992

Continue the story, saying what happened after the father visited the District Office and returned home.

- Make the father the focus of your story.
- Use what you have learned about his life, his family and their circumstances.
- Write between a page and a page and a half.

● Writing a leaflet

When you are writing a leaflet, you must think about the layout and language you need to use. Look at leaflets in doctors' waiting rooms, travel agents, railway and bus stations, and so on. You will find that they have a clear layout, so that your eye is taken straight to the important information. They are also written in simple, straightforward language, so that the information is easy to understand. You will find some more ideas to help you write leaflets on pages 121–22.

Exercise 1

This exercise, and the one that follows, can help you to practise writing a leaflet. Here is a collection of details and opinions concerning the effects of climate change in the Arctic region. Read carefully the passage and then complete the task which follows.

The Arctic

Facts and figures

- **66° 33'N:** The lower limit of the Arctic, strictly defined.
- **30 million km²** of marine and terrestrial ecosystems.
- **Polar bears** live in the Arctic – it's their only home. Penguins do not live in the Arctic.
- **4 million people** live within the Arctic Circle.
- **–40°C (–40°F):** Average winter temperature in some parts of the Arctic.
- **The smallest ocean** in the world is the Arctic Ocean.
- **8 countries** are recognized as Arctic states.

Consisting of deep ocean covered by drifting pack ice and surrounded by continents and archipelagos around the Earth's North Pole, the Arctic is the planet's largest and least fragmented inhabited region.

But by the end of this century, the Arctic will be a very different place. Temperatures are warming more than twice as fast as they are for the planet as a whole. Sea ice is melting. Arctic wildlife and people are beginning to live altered lives. ▶▶

How is the Arctic affected by climate change?

Climate change is faster and more severe in the Arctic than in most of the rest of the world. The Arctic is warming at a rate of almost twice the global average.

Summer sea ice is disappearing

The sea ice that is a critical component of Arctic marine ecosystems is projected to disappear in the summer within a generation.

- Arctic sea ice has decreased 14% since the 1970s.
- In 2012, Arctic sea ice extent hit the lowest level ever recorded, breaking the previous record set in 2007.
- By 2040, summer sea ice could be limited to the northern coast of Greenland and Canada. This is the Last Ice Area.

The Arctic is warming faster than the rest of the world

Why? Shiny ice and snow reflect a high proportion of the sun's energy into space. As the Arctic loses snow and ice, bare rock and water absorb more and more of the sun's energy, making it ever warmer. This is called the 'albedo effect'.

A small temperature shift can have enormous implications

Even an increase of 2°C could be too much. A slight shift in temperature, bringing averages above the freezing point, will completely alter the character of the region.

- Polar bears could become extinct by the end of this century if there is an almost complete loss of summer sea ice cover.
- As snow and ice melt, the ability of the Arctic to reflect heat back to space is reduced, accelerating the overall rate of global warming.
- Some arctic fisheries will disappear.
- We are likely to see more forest fires and storm damage to coastal communities in the Arctic.
- Glaciers, sea ice and tundra will melt, contributing to global sea level rises.
- A warmer Arctic could halt the Gulf Stream, which brings warmer water and weather to north-western Europe.

How will plants and animals be affected?

A warmer climate will have a major impact on the Arctic and result in major changes for plant and animal species. Melting permafrost will cause large quantities of methane and carbon dioxide to be released, boosting global temperatures already on the rise.

- There will be major changes in the composition of plant communities. Southern plant species will migrate northwards and suppress existing plants, affecting the species that depend on them. Insects responsible for pollination are one example of the coexistence that will be threatened.
- Changes in access to nutritious plants (both in time and space) will be decisive for herbivores such as musk oxen and reindeer.
- Changes in the success of birds' nesting patterns will be decisive for how migratory birds cope with climate change.
- The future for fish stocks depends on sea temperatures and algae blooms that are an essential source of food. Arctic waters will become more acidic as CO_2 uptake increases, negatively affecting some organisms.
- Retreating sea ice is already a major threat to most seal species and walruses.

These predictions aside, scientists cannot describe exactly how climate change will affect the Arctic. We will only obtain precise knowledge about climate change effects as they occur, by which time it will be too late. Only immediate cuts in greenhouse gas emissions can prevent catastrophic and irreversible change, so action is required now.

Adapted from WWF

Write a leaflet for an environmental organisation aimed at raising people's awareness of the effects of climate change in the Arctic and asking for support. The leaflet will be delivered to people's homes.
Use the information in the passage as a basis for your writing. You may also add ideas of your own.

Exercise 2

The following task refers to the passage 'Protecting children from pool accidents' on pages 76–77. Read again this passage and use it as a source of information for your leaflet.

Write a short guide for young children advising them on how they should behave around swimming pools.

- You should set your points out clearly.
- Remember who your intended audience is.

Write about a page.

Study tip

If you choose to write a travel guide for your coursework portfolio, you should apply the same techniques as for writing a leaflet.

6 Writing compositions

Most English Language syllabuses will include one paper which tests your ability to write in response to both directed and imaginative writing tasks. Some syllabuses will test this under timed examination conditions, some will test these skills through coursework tasks and some, like Cambridge IGCSE First Language English, will allow you to choose whether you follow an examination or coursework route. This chapter looks at the special skills you need for the examination route and Chapter 7 looks at the coursework route. For *all* your writing, you will need to show that you can:

- articulate experience and express what is thought, felt and imagined
- sequence facts, ideas and opinions
- use a range of appropriate vocabulary
- use register appropriate to audience and context
- make accurate use of spelling, punctuation and grammar.

You will almost certainly practise writing compositions during your course. However, there are some important differences between this type of continuous writing and the compositions that you will be asked to write in an examination. Although the tasks are similar, in an examination you have extra challenges to face, and this chapter will try to help you meet them.

- **Challenge 1: You don't know what the topics will be.**
  You will not have had the opportunity to prepare the subject of your writing in advance because you won't know what you will be asked to write about until you open the question paper.
- **Challenge 2: You have to write within a time limit.**
  In an examination, you must complete your composition within a certain period of time: usually one hour, or one hour and thirty minutes.
- **Challenge 3: Writing to a particular length.**
  The examination paper includes a guideline telling you how long your composition should be. Does it matter if it's too long or too short?
- **Challenge 4: There's only one chance to get it right.**
  When you write compositions as part of your schoolwork you have the opportunity to produce a first draft, which you can revise and improve until you are satisfied that the final product is as good as you can possibly make it. Under examination conditions, the time limit makes it impossible to draft several versions, but you should try to allow time for certain important checks. We all make technical errors of spelling, punctuation and expression at times, and such errors are much more likely to occur when you are writing under these conditions. Stress can lead to mistakes! It is important to check through your work so that you don't lose marks unnecessarily for this kind of error.

Some practical guidelines

In the continuous writing part of an examination you will be required to write both a piece of directed writing and a composition. We have dealt with directed writing in Chapter 5; in this section we will be looking specifically at issues concerned with the composition task.

Meeting Challenge 1: choosing from the topics on the paper

From experience throughout your course you should have a good idea of the **type** of composition you are best at writing. This should help you to choose which topic to write about in an examination. This may not be the topic that immediately looks most attractive – remember that you only have to write about 350–450 words, and if you choose a 'favourite' topic you may find that you have too much to say and your answer is in danger of becoming too long and unstructured. An examination paper will contain different types of compositions for you to choose from. There will usually be **narrative** and **descriptive** topics.

Study tips

Choose your topic on the basis of two points.

1 Your skills – think carefully about which type of writing you are most successful at (especially under timed conditions). Think about this before the examination so that you can make the best possible choice when you see the paper.
2 Your interest in the topic and any experience of your own that enables you to comment on it – **but** still make sure you focus really closely on the question. Your own experience can be an inspiration, but don't let it become a distraction!

Meeting Challenge 2: writing within a time limit

The time limit means that planning is even more important than usual, not less! Make a skeleton plan of the main points that you intend to include before you start to write. Doing this will show you whether you have enough to say about the topic, as well as providing you with a paragraph structure. It is worth spending ten minutes on your plan.

Study tips

1 Don't write full sentences in your plan, just brief notes. Note down one key idea per paragraph, backed up by very brief notes on how you will explain or argue that idea. Overall, five to eight paragraphs should be adequate, plus …
2 Your **conclusion**. Don't forget to include this in your plan; it is a very good idea to know how you intend to finish the composition before you start to write it!
3 You could use a spider diagram to sort out your ideas for your composition. There are examples on pages 65 and 66.

Meeting Challenge 3: writing to a particular length

The advice about the number of words you should write is there as a guideline for you, but it is not an absolute requirement. It is possible to write *slightly less* than the suggested length (say, 40–50 words less) and still gain a top grade if the expression, content and structure of your composition are of the required standard. Similarly, you are not likely to be penalised if you *exceed* the suggested word limit, but by doing so you are increasing the chance of making careless slips and errors which may reduce your potential mark. (Example 1 on pages 112–14 is a very good example of a student successfully writing more than required.)

If you plan your composition carefully, staying clearly focused on the topic, you should not have much difficulty in keeping to the suggested length.

Meeting Challenge 4: make time to check your work!

Try to keep at least ten minutes at the end of the examination to check your work. Check:

- spelling
- punctuation
- paragraphing
- tenses.

(Chapter 4 outlines some key points to remember on these aspects of your work.) A few mistakes are inevitable but a large number of mistakes will affect your mark. Finally, **make sure your writing is clearly legible** – if you write a brilliant piece that can't be read, it won't score the marks you deserve.

Writing the composition

Quite simply, the main concern of those reading your work will be to assess how effectively you can convey your thoughts about your chosen topic by using written Standard English. Your readers will want to be interested in what you have written. The more easily they can understand your ideas, the higher the mark you are likely to gain. Always try to see your work from the reader's point of view!

Expressing your ideas

Remember that you will be assessed for **how you have expressed your ideas** as well as for **what you have written**. Examinations test your **ability to communicate** in written English; they do not test the level of your imagination and creativity. Look back at Chapter 4 for some basic reminders about how to structure your work and keep the level of accuracy in your writing as high as possible. Below are a few more guidelines which are particularly useful when writing compositions.

Use paragraphs logically

Make sure that your writing is divided into paragraphs and that the paragraphs are logically developed.

The opening paragraph should provide a valuable introduction, both to the topic and to the person writing about it; it should set the tone for the composition and make clear the direction it is going to take.

The middle section of the composition should be clearly structured and logically sequenced.

Your conclusion should give evidence of being clearly planned for and the composition should finish with a positive conclusion.

The more simply, the more clearly and the more precisely you communicate your ideas to the reader, the higher your mark will be.

Write in complete sentences

While you are writing your composition, always try to **think in complete sentences**; never start to write a sentence until you know how it is going to finish.

Make sure you use full stops to separate sentences correctly. You must be able to show a secure ability to separate sentences correctly in order to achieve a grade C or above for your composition.

Take care with punctuation

A common error is to confuse the use of commas with the use of full stops. Other serious punctuation errors result from misunderstandings about how to use the apostrophe and how to use inverted commas to punctuate direct speech. Make sure you know how to use these punctuation marks correctly and check them when you have finished your composition.

Check your spelling

You will be penalised if you misspell, or confuse, basic vocabulary (*there/their*; *too/to/two*; *quite/quiet*, etc.), or if you spell simple words in more than one incorrect way. Nevertheless, you should not let your worries about spelling prevent you from using what you know is the best word for the job. A reader will usually recognise the word you intend to use, even if it is incorrectly spelt. Although it may be noted as a spelling error, you are likely to be given credit for choosing and knowing how to use the word in the first place.

Features of a good composition

You will be relieved to know that you are not likely to have a mark deducted for every technical error that you make. As mentioned earlier, your composition will be marked by impression and the reader will balance the positive and negative qualities of your writing in his/her mind. The main positive features for which you will be credited are:

1 **The ability to structure and organise your ideas clearly.**
  A well-controlled, well-developed composition with a positive opening and a strong conclusion will usually be well received.
2 **A wide range of appropriately used and precise vocabulary.**
  This does not mean that you should fill your composition with the longest and most complicated words you can think of. On the contrary, it means that you should have a clear understanding of what you are going to say and a good vocabulary, so that you can choose the right word to convey the exact shade of meaning that you want.
3 **A good range and variety of sentence types and structures.**
  This helps to avoid monotony in your writing. Try not to let every sentence take the same form, or begin each paragraph with sentences of the same pattern. To do well in your composition you need to show evidence that you can handle complex sentences confidently. However, the ability to use short, simple, direct sentences when your composition requires it is also important. So, vary the length and type of your sentences (compound, complex, simple) to suit your meaning.

But *what* do I write?

We have been concentrating on *how* rather than *what* to write. You may be wondering about content. Content is certainly important, but some students tend to worry too much about it and create unnecessary problems for themselves. The main points to remember are:

1 **Be realistic.**
  You do not have time to write a novel during an examination and you will not be expected to do so. So, don't make things more difficult for yourself by trying to think of obscure or totally original ideas: the originality of your writing will be found mainly in the way you express yourself.

2 Keep it clear and simple.

What you write should be well planned, carefully structured and organised, and clearly focused on the topic you have chosen. Your main intention should be to think how best to use the language to put across your ideas as clearly and as vividly as you can. Keep what you write simple and manageable; base your content on and within your own experience and you won't go far wrong.

Examples of students' work

Here are three sample student compositions for a Cambridge IGCSE First Language English examination. Read them through carefully. You might like to decide what grades you think they would have been awarded and why before you read the teacher's analysis that follows.

The original spellings and punctuation have been retained and major errors of spelling, punctuation and expression have been indicated. **It is important to remember, however, that in an examination you will be credited for positive merits of style, vocabulary and so on, as much as penalised for errors.** For this reason, it is unlikely that every error made by a student would be indicated and the marking of the following examples reflects this principle.

Example 1

> Write a story in which severe weather conditions play a significant part.

Key

Errors of expression

Spelling/ punctuation errors

wrong word ('secret')

repetition

The perpetual wailing of the Hawaiian winds was no novelty to the professor; a veteran scientist whose name was renound in the field of meteorological studies. Seated on a brown leather eighteenth-century chair, the hollow cries of wind outside were a constant reminder that weather was supreme. Though the powerful evening breeze could uproot the studiest of trees, however, it could not touch the thin delicate clouds of smoke rising from Professor Dean's pipe, a thought at which he could not suppress a smile. It was to him, ironic that he was the creator of the 'Typhoon Eye', a secretive government project under his authority. Outside the complexe, atop a remote mountain on the island of Waikiki, in the Hawaiian Archipelago, the skies darkened as small droplets of cold rain began to fall on the island from the heavens above. At sea, some distance away, a rumble of thunder of thunder was heard, an omen of events to come.

Seated in his office, in serene relaxation, as thick smoke escaped from his lips, a loud series of knocks at his door revived the tired Prof. Dean from his quasi-slumber. 'Come in', he called with a bored tone of voice.

The hinges creaked with a dull sound as a tall, youthful figure entered in the office clad in thick clothes and a clean white labcoat.

'Oh, what is it, my boy?' inquired the professor without turning to face his guest.

'I just came to tell you, sir, that our guest from Washington is anxious to activate the device' replied the young assistant.

'Are all preparations complete?'

'They are, sir.'

'Well then', continued the arthritic, greying scientist, 'I'll be there shortly.'

With a nod, the youth left, carefully shutting the door as he egressed. Removing his cashmere jumper and preparing to don more formal attire, Prof. Dean glanced outside his window. He saw a tangled mass of tropical trees, swaying in the wind. Evidently a hurricane of some sort was indeed approaching.

'Welcome to Command Central. Please Indentify yourself.'

Walking through the dimly lit corridoors as he was observed by the highly disciplined guards which flanked the hallway, Prof. Dean reached into his pocket and inserted his access card into a brightly-lit panel.

humorous 'Thank you, Professor Gordon H H Dean ...' replied the wall in a mechanistic tone of voice. The thick titanium doors shuddered open. Walking through them, he entered a new environment all together. at Command Central, several dozen scientists and researchers were hastily preparing for the prototype test. Moving back and forth between the project itself, a huge device named the 'Typhoon Eye' and the terminals of advanced computers which controlled it, the men moved with almost robotic efficiency. No voice could clearly be heard, sideline conversations and idle chattering darted chaotically across the room.

'Professor, you're here at last!' cried an enthusiastic diplomat seated some distance away.

Emerging from the trance the mayhem of the room had caused him, Dean recognised him as Murray Bunton, their liaison to Washington.

'We're ready to activate the device!' he said as the room fell silent.

After a brief pause, Dean moved towards the main control module and pressed the large button labelled 'BEGIN'.

effective short sentence Immediately the device shook and emitted many sounds. ✓

Standing dumb in awed silence, the scientists let out a collective cheer.

'This is a great moment for mankind,' whispered Bunton, 'Now, at last, men control the weather! With this device, mankind can manipulate the elements to our advantage!'

The atmosphere slowly ionised the surrounding area, releasing strange types of energy in all directions.

After toasting to their success with glasses of Martini, the group retired for the night, expecting a clear sky the next day.

Awoken from his sleep, Dean stumbled out of bed to replace his clothes. Looking at his clock with sluggish, blood-shot eyes, it read five o'clock in the morning.

'Hurry, Professor!' came the voice again.

Rushing through the security doors, his eyes were greeted by a room of haunting silence, the only sounds a series of murmurs from the main control panel operators. Outside a terrifying clap of thunder roared across the ocean.

'What's happened?' Inquired the professor, highly concerned despite his condition. There he was told that far from dissipating the storms, Typhoon Eye had had the reverse effect. Tropical cyclone 'Lethea' was now being drawn to Waikiki.

'How could this happen?' demanded Bunton, still half-dressed.

Silence was his only reply.

Key

Errors of expression

Spelling/ punctuation errors

> Some time later, while the weather outside continued to worsen, Dean sat down to drink a final cup of malt whisky. The room was deserted, a collection of empty chairs and dysfunctional machines with paper strewn al over the floor. And of course, there was me, the youthful scientist who had summoned the Professor to Command Central. I had stayed behind too, when offered a chance to evacuate. I could not deny my own responsibility for this disaster.
>
> Outside, the cyclone had once again grown in strength, and had wiped out everything in the Hawaiian Islands.
>
> The storm would remain here, its source of strength was this island, as it had now been polarised and filled with this energy. The storm would grow, slowly but surely gaining strength, eventually covering the entire planet.
>
> Having gone to fetch some coffee, I heard a sudden gun shot, and a dull thud. I collapsed in a corner and wept. I could not bear to see the professor's corpse. Outside, the storm began to tear the building apart. I would soon be dead. As the outside breeze slowly infiltrated the room from holes in the roof, I pondered on man's underestimation of the wind. And now I realised that I had as well. ✓

Teacher's analysis: This composition is a long (946 words) but well-sustained narrative. This is obviously written by a student who enjoys writing and has relished the opportunity of entertaining the reader. It opens forcefully, and immediately engages the reader's attention. The vocabulary is wide, varied, ambitious and fully appropriate. The writer uses a good range of sentence structures and types: there are well-controlled complex sentences, for example:

> Outside the complex, atop a remote mountain on the island of Waikiki, in the Hawaiian Archipelago, the skies darkened as small droplets of cold rain began to fall on the island from the heavens above.

and some effectively used short, simple sentences, for example: 'Silence was his only reply.'

The writer has chosen to write a long and involved narrative and does so with confidence. There is no doubt that this writer is consciously trying to impress the reader with his/her mastery of the English language and he/she does so in particular through a plentiful use of adjectives ('The arthritic, greying scientist') and a deliberate use of literary language ('Preparing to don more formal attire'), although, in places, this approach is somewhat overdone. It is an extremely confident piece of writing; there is a clear narrative flow which is emphasised by the controlled use of long and short paragraphs for effect.

Direct speech is used convincingly and correctly punctuated, apart from a tendency to misplace commas ('"This is a great moment for mankind", whispered Bunton'), and the writer is not afraid to risk a humorous touch ('replied the wall'). The composition is not without blemishes, both of spelling (renound, complexe, studiest) and expression ('Seated in his office … a loud series of knocks') but these weaknesses are very much the product of first-draft writing and the writer's ambition. They do not impede the reader's understanding and are more than compensated for by the composition's many merits, not least the way it remains clearly focused on the title throughout. The story is original and well developed.

Perhaps the most disappointing part of the composition is the end: the writer could obviously have written more had there been more time, but what is here is a most impressive achievement for the limited time available, and it is likely that this piece of writing would be assessed as a secure **grade** A response.

Example 2

'The only worthwhile thing in life is going to parties.' What are your views?

I reckon this statement is rubbish. Many factors influence me in beleiving this way. As much as partying is fun it can equally be exhausting and unhealthy in some cases. By, keeping on partying, you are causing a huge deteriaration in your health which could inturn be quite life threatening. Certainly almost every party will have some alchoholic beverages in entertain it's customers, and definitely, if you are a drinker, you would'nt hesitate from staying away from the booze. It is just almost impossible to do so and therefore you would'nt refrain.

two words not one

At the age of fifteen, partying may seem the most worthwhile thing to do in life as an adoloscent, but looking ahead to the future, it does indeed seem quite bleak for someone partying all the time at this age.

A student that party's all day is certainly not going to get good marks or grades in their examination, and this inturn will reflect upon the student's causes. A bit of common sense and awareness of the present situation is all that is needed to realise exactly what the main objective is at this point of our lives. Studies should unduly be the priority right now Ofcourse socialising is another aspect of life that is quite important as inter-personal communications and relationships could be demanded all our lives, but is it really the priority right now? Do our social commitments have to overshadow our whole future in front of us? I would say not. When the time comes to party, you can party but it is definitely not the only worthwhile thing in life at the adolescent age of fifteen.

wrong word
two words not one

Other than the health factor and the education factor, I would believe that partying would be joyful. But only someone who is either peripherally blind or intellectually numb would say that it is the ONLY worthwhile thing to do in life. How many years will you party for? Is it going to get you anywhere in life? I would'nt think so. 'Going to parties' may seem as 'fun' at the time but in the long term, I really doubt as to how far in life it is really going to help you.

Also, most parties occur during nights and drag on till midnight or past. This will be a huge drain of energy from the party goer's part. It is definitely worth it at the time, but the after-effects are rather disturbing and uncomfortable.

Is it really worth wasting your whole life that way? Especially at this age, I would reckon, that it is much more of a use to prioritise as to what is worthwhile now, now instead of regretting it in the future.

Teacher's analysis: This composition begins with a forceful and unambiguous opening which is expressed directly but is not entirely appropriate in its tone of voice: 'I reckon this statement is rubbish.' As the composition develops, it becomes clear that the writing is poorly organised.

The writer possesses quite a wide vocabulary, but it is not always used with precision ('Studies should unduly be the priority right now.'). The word the student should have used is 'undoubtedly' or 'indubitably'.

Some statements, which sound linguistically quite impressive if read superficially ('inter-personal communications and relationships could be demanded all our lives') do not make clear sense on closer reading.

The development of the writer's argument is uncertain and lacking in cohesion; the ideas, although potentially interesting, are underdeveloped. The end of the penultimate paragraph is a good example of this; more details could have been included as to how the after-effects are disturbing and uncomfortable – the writer's meaning has not been made entirely clear to the reader.

There are several technical errors of spelling (beleiving, alchoholic, adolescent) and expression ('"Going to parties" may seem as fun.').

The inappropriate tone of the opening sentence has already been referred to and this over-colloquial approach appears at other points throughout the writing, where it sits rather inconsistently with some over-formal expressions ('Many factors influence me'), with the result that the work lacks a clear focus on the audience.

The reader is required to re-read paragraphs to understand fully what the writer is trying to say, with the result that communication becomes blurred. The whole of the third paragraph is a good example of this.

This piece of writing is an ambitious attempt but, in this case, the writer lacks the linguistic security to communicate the ideas clearly. The ending is also disappointing as the writer has run out of time and has not managed to produce a satisfactory conclusion. This student has made a fundamental mistake: he/she has chosen to write a difficult type of composition (an argumentative one) and has made the task harder than it need be. Had he/she chosen a descriptive or narrative topic, the outcome would most probably have been more successful, as less time would have had to be spent on constructing arguments and more time would have been available to concentrate on making the most of the writer's positive merits of vocabulary. The material which was written is unlikely to gain higher than a **grade** E.

Example 3

> 'Hidden Treasure'
> Write in any way you like about this topic.

Key

Errors of expression

Spelling/
punctuation errors

two words not one

'Runners for the 800 metre race, please go to zone 3,' announced one of the judges at the scoring table.

I knew that was my call. Once I stood up, I hurriedly turned to a slim, tall girl called Mary Anne. (Eversince) she joined the training team, I had this bad feeling and imagined that I would be beaten by her.

As I walked boldly, I looked up at the cloudy sky. It had such a dirty grey colour. But I told myself no matter what the weather was like it wouldn't influence me because I was going to win!

'Can you all stand separately? The race is about to start,' shouted a woman with a grim face. I found myself in an excited crowd. Out of them, my eyes found themselves on Mary Anne who was quietly doing warm ups.

√THUMP! THUMP!

My heart was hammering at my ribs. Why was I nervous? I had success in numerous races before, and this would not be an exception.

CONCENTRATE, EVA, YOU MUST WIN THIS RACE!

'On your marks, get set . . .'

YOU ARE DEAD, EVA.

. . . go!'

All I saw was darkness. I opened my eyes and found myself running as fast as I possibly could.

DRIP! DROP! DRIP! DROP!

I felt waterdrops. It wet my dried throat when I opened my mouth to breathe. Amazingly, the rain drops gave me a rush of energy. I was on the road again. Not only did I keep a good pace, I ran faster and faster. The track in front of me seemed like a mile long. I ran all I could towards the finish line. Suddenly I felt a great pain in the ankle. I kneeled down desperately and found out that I twisted the ankle while running. Other runners ran pass me and I saw Mary Anne had this worried look on her face as she ran pass. It was hopeless, now, even though there was only 100 metres left to the finish line, I cannot possibly finish it?'!

'were' not 'was'
inconsistent tenses – was (past), cannot (present)

Before, I felt like I was going to cry. I saw a shadow, a person, coming towards me in the rain. The person's hands helped me up and I saw the face just above mine was Mary Anne's! She kindly comforted me and said, 'Come on, Eva! You can do it!' With her help I was able to topple along and before long, I finally reach the finish line. It was like a door to paradise! If it wasn't Mary Anne's encouragement and help, I wouldn't have done it. From this memorable event, Mary Anne and I became very close friends as I found after talking to her that we were a lot in common.

wrong word ('had')

I realised that I have gained a treasure, it was not the winning medal or any prize but a caring and trustworthy friend.

This was the hidden treasure that I have never known before and I am so glad that I found it!

Teacher's analysis: This composition opens confidently and leads into a controlled, well-structured story which develops towards a definite conclusion. There are positive merits in its structure, particularly the skilful way in which the details of the race are woven into the action of the story ('YOU ARE DEAD, EVA.' '… go!'). The story is sufficiently clear to engage the reader's interest and to sustain it. There is quite a wide range of vocabulary which is appropriately used ('rush of energy', 'I was able to topple along'). The writer's expression is secure and confident enough for him/her to concentrate on selecting words and phrases which are designed to appeal to and interest the reader.

However, despite its many good qualities, this composition lacks a variety of style. Overall, there is not a great variety of sentence types and structures, and the writer tends to rely on short, simple sentences. It would appear that the writer is using these as a result of linguistic limitations rather than deliberately to create a sense of tension and excitement.

Overall, this composition is the work of a writer who is aware of his/her limitations and strengths and, in general, does not try to go beyond them. Assessing this composition involves balancing the good and less good qualities. On the whole, the good qualities outweigh the others and the composition was assessed as a solid **grade C**.

Practise writing a composition

Now that you have looked at some sample student compositions, here are some titles which you can use for practice. To help you, we have indicated next to each topic whether it is narrative, descriptive or argumentative. (In some cases, you will notice, the same topic could lend itself to more than one approach.) Two of the topics are *discursive*, which means you can approach the question in any way you choose.

1 'Television is a bad influence; it stops people thinking and ruins family life.' What are your views about the value of television? (Argumentative)
2 Which is your favourite day of the week and why? (Descriptive)
3 Write a story beginning with the words 'The noise was growing louder and louder,' and ending 'And then there was silence.' (Narrative)
4 What have you taught yourself that is not taught at your school? (Argumentative/Descriptive)
5 Do we spend too much time watching sports instead of playing them? (Argumentative)
6 Describe a place you know well at two different times of the day. (Descriptive)
7 'Castles in the Air'. Write in any way you like about this topic. (Discursive)
8 Write a story called 'The Empty House'. (Narrative)
9 'Decisions'. Write in any way you like about this topic. (Discursive)
10 What do you think are the greatest challenges facing young people today? (Argumentative)
11 Describe your favourite shop and some of the people who work there. (Descriptive)
12 'A Journey I Will Never Forget'. (Narrative)

Study tip

You can plan your compositions in different ways. For example, you can produce a straightforward skeleton plan or use a spider diagram. Examples of both types of plans are shown below and opposite – they relate to the first two questions in the list above. You could use them as the basis for writing your own practice composition, and then as models for writing your own plans for other compositions. Remember, the points in each plan should provide you with the topic sentences for your paragraphs. It is up to you to add the details which make the paragraphs interesting!

Examples of composition plans

Skeleton plan for Question 1: 'Television is a bad influence; it stops people thinking and ruins family life.'

Introduction: General comments on TV; its popularity, ubiquity; it is now a focal point in most households; it has become a major part of our lives.

Points against: It stops conversation and limits communication among people; it can cause family arguments over what to watch; it stops families doing more constructive things together; many of the most popular programmes are superficial; it is very easy to become addicted to certain programmes (soap operas, etc.) with the result that studies take a back seat; it tells you what to think.

Points for: It provides company for people who are on their own; it brings news and sporting events direct into the home and allows you to feel as though you are present at them even if they are on the other side of the world; it has some educational value – in fact, something can be learnt from most programmes; it can develop and refine one's analytical powers; it provides a ready topic of conversation with your friends.

Conclusion: Sum up the main points made above, refer to own experience and that of friends and state conclusion about how much truth there is in the topic statement.

Spider diagram plan for Question 2: Which is your favourite day of the week and why?

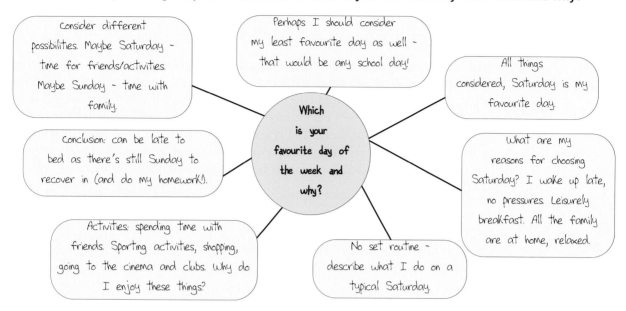

Consider different possibilities. Maybe Saturday – time for friends/activities. Maybe Sunday – time with family.

Perhaps I should consider my least favourite day as well – that would be any school day!

All things considered, Saturday is my favourite day.

Conclusion: can be late to bed as there's still Sunday to recover in (and do my homework!).

Which is your favourite day of the week and why?

What are my reasons for choosing Saturday? I wake up late, no pressures. Leisurely breakfast. All the family are at home, relaxed.

Activities: spending time with friends. Sporting activities, shopping, going to the cinema and clubs. Why do I enjoy these things?

No set routine – describe what I do on a typical Saturday.

Written coursework

Why do coursework?

As an alternative to the written examination, you may produce up to three pieces of continuous writing and submit them as a coursework portfolio. But, if you have this option available, why should you do coursework? Isn't it easier just to sit down for two hours and write? Not necessarily! If you do coursework you have the opportunity to plan and check your work, and you can draft and redraft the piece of writing. You can be sure that, at the end of the process, your work is as good as you can possibly make it. Remember that for *all* your writing, you will need to show that you can:

- articulate experience and express what is thought, felt and imagined
- sequence facts, ideas and opinions
- use a range of appropriate vocabulary
- use register appropriate to audience and context
- make accurate use of spelling, punctuation and grammar.

What do you have to do?

The syllabus requirements for Coursework (Component 4) for Cambridge IGCSE First Language English are that candidates submit a portfolio of **three** assignments, each of about 500–800 words. The assignments may be completed in any order and are:

- **Assignment 1:** a piece of informative, analytical and/or argumentative writing (factual)
- **Assignment 2:** a piece of descriptive and/or narrative writing (expressive)
- **Assignment 3:** a response to a text or texts chosen by the Centre. The text(s) should contain facts, opinions and arguments. You will be required to respond by selecting, analysing and evaluating content of the text(s). This assignment will also test your reading skills.

Now let's consider these requirements.

Length

It is likely that examination syllabuses will suggest an optimum number of words for each question (e.g. 500–800 words). Will you be penalised if you write more or fewer words than this? The answer is 'no'! Your pieces of writing need to be as long as is necessary to complete the task and to demonstrate your range of writing skills. Remember that you are not awarded marks just because you have written a lot; in fact, writing that has started well can sometimes lose its effectiveness and get worse the longer it goes on.

Coursework assignments

Doing coursework gives you the chance to demonstrate your skills in writing in different ways and styles. In everyday life we write for a variety of reasons. We might be required to write formal reports during our working life. We might be asked to write an article for a community newsletter, possibly an account of something particularly interesting we have done, perhaps a funny anecdote. We might have the job of writing the monthly newsletter for a club or group. In each of these situations we would have a different audience and a different purpose, so we would need to write each piece in a different style.

This is why you are asked to write three different pieces; it reflects the reality of how writing is used in everyday life. When you are choosing the different pieces to include in your coursework portfolio, remember this point and think:

- Who am I writing for in each piece?
- What is the purpose of each piece?
- Am I choosing pieces that are different from each other?

Assignment 1: the factual piece

You must write an informative, analytical and/or argumentative piece. It could be in the form of an essay, but it might be more interesting to choose a different format, such as a letter, a report, or the words of a talk (there is advice on writing each of these in Chapter 5). Some other ideas include:

- a publicity handout or leaflet
- a set of instructions explaining how to perform a task
- a programme for a cultural event
- a travel guide to a place or area that you know
- an account of a particular real-life experience.

Below is an example of just one type of informative writing: an information leaflet which you could use as a model for your own writing. Think about: how information is made to stand out; the order the information is given in and why; the vocabulary used, and so on. Also think about the tone of the leaflet and how it helps to emphasise the information that is being passed on.

Example of an informative piece

The following leaflet was produced by the pharmacy chain UniChem and was sent out to pharmacies, doctors' surgeries and other health clinics. It has been carefully written and designed to make the information accessible.

Sports injuries

The information is broken up into short sections, each with a large heading. There is plenty of space around the headings, to make them stand out.

The language is simple and clear, and short sentences are used. This helps to make the information easy to understand.

Grazes and skin burns
These occur as a result of friction.

- **A graze** (abrasion) is a superficial skin wound commonly caused by a sliding fall. The top skin layers are scraped off, leaving a raw, painful area. The palms of the hands or knees are common sites for grazes. Foreign particles sometimes become embedded in the grazed area and pose an infection risk.
- **Friction burns** of the skin may be due to rope burns or sliding falls on synthetic sports surfaces.

First aid treatment for grazes and friction burns of the skin involves careful cleaning of the wound, preferably by rinsing dirty grazes under gently running water. Glass or grit may be gently picked off the surface of the graze, but do not attempt to remove embedded debris – seek medical treatment. After rinsing, cover the wound with sterile gauze, clean the surrounding area and apply a plaster or light dressing.

Cramp
Cramp is a painful muscle spasm that may arise following any exercise, but particularly swimming and running. Muscle spasm occurs when muscles contract for too long, or

when profuse sweating causes water and salt loss. Lactic acid accumulates in muscles following strenuous exercise and this also causes cramp. Massage of the affected muscle often helps to relieve the spasm and pain.

First aid

First aid: following an injury to the soft tissues, including sprains, deep bruising and muscular injuries, first aiders should follow the R.I.C.E. procedure as follows: **R**est the affected part: **I**ce, apply a cold pad to the injured part. Alternative 'ice packs' could include a bag of frozen peas or vegetables, wrapped in a tea-towel. **C**ompress the injured part by means of a supportive bandage. **E**levate the part that is injured.

Prevention: many sports-related injuries may be prevented by:

- wearing correct footwear for your particular sport
- replacing worn sports shoes
- practising your technique and obtaining professional guidance if possible
- wearing protective clothing or equipment (where applicable)
- warming up before strenuous exercise and cooling down afterwards
- devising your own loosening up routine to increase blood flow to the muscles, allowing sufficient time for old injuries to heal.

Always read the label.

You can obtain professional advice and a variety of treatments at your UniChem Community pharmacy.

From UniChem Pharmacies

Bullet points are used to help readers pick out relevant details.

What should I write?

There may be a topic in which you have a burning interest and you may feel that you can sit down and get going without any preparation. Don't! Doing coursework gives you the important opportunity to do your research and make sure that all the facts you use are 100 per cent accurate. So get your facts together and sort through them before you start.

If a topic doesn't spring to mind immediately, then there is a whole range of sources to give you ideas. You might get your inspiration from:

- a programme on the television
- a discussion of a topic suggested by your teacher in class
- something you have read
- something you have heard on the radio.

The text opposite is an extract from a book in which the author describes a school which he established. He explains the educational philosophy on which the school was based. The ideas contained in this extract could start you thinking about issues relating to education and be a springboard for a piece of writing on a related topic, such as:

- If you had the power to do so, what changes would you make to the education system in your country and why?
- Describe your ideal school and how it should be run.
- Write an 'insider's guide' for students starting their first year at your school.

When my first wife and I began the school, we had one main idea: to make the school fit the child – instead of making the child fit the school.

I had taught in ordinary schools for many years. I knew the other way well. I knew it was all wrong. It was wrong because it was based on an adult conception of what a child should be and how a child should learn. The other way dated from the days when psychology was still an unknown science.

Well, we set out to make a school in which we should allow children freedom to be themselves. In order to do this, we had to renounce all discipline, all direction, all suggestion, all moral training, all religious instruction. We have been called brave, but it did not require courage. All it required was what we had – a complete belief in the child as a good, not an evil, being. For over forty years, this belief in the goodness of the child has never wavered; it rather has become a final faith.

My view is that a child is innately wise and realistic. If left to himself without any adult suggestion of any kind, he will develop as far as he is capable of developing. Logically, Summerhill is a place in which people who have the innate ability and wish to be scholars will be scholars; while those who are only fit to sweep the streets will sweep the streets. But we have not produced a street cleaner so far. Nor do I write this snobbishly, for I would rather see a school produce a happy street cleaner than a neurotic scholar.

What is Summerhill like? Well, for one thing, lessons are optional. Children can go to them or stay away from them – for years if they want to. There is a timetable – but only for the teachers.

The children have classes usually according to their age, but sometimes according to their interests. We have no new methods of teaching, because we do not consider that teaching in itself matters very much. Whether a school has or has not a special method for teaching long division is of no significance, for long division is of no importance except to those who want to learn it. And the child who wants to learn long division will learn it no matter how it is taught.

Children who come to Summerhill as kindergarteners attend lessons from the beginning of their stay; but pupils from other schools vow that they will never attend any beastly lessons again at any time. They play and cycle and get in people's way, but they fight shy of lessons. This sometimes goes on for months. The recovery time is proportionate to the hatred their last school gave them.

From *Summerhill* by A.S. Neill

You will have noticed that the three suggested tasks based on reading this passage allow you either to write **analytically** and **argumentatively** or to write in an **informative** way. The third task also gives you a suggested **audience** for your writing and a possible **format**. Remember that you need to write in a register which is appropriate to both your audience and the required format. When you are drafting your coursework for this type of writing, you may find it helpful to decide on a specific audience and format before you start developing your ideas. For example, you could expand on the second of the suggested tasks by setting it as a radio discussion between two people with opposing ideas about how a school should be run. This would allow you to present two sides of the picture and also allow you to demonstrate your skills at writing dialogue.

> **Study tips**
>
> 1 Make sure that you use your research and make it belong to you. Don't just copy the information. In your planning make sure that you get the points in the order you want. If you fail to do this, it will look as if you are just copying your sources rather than the work being your own.
> 2 You should always list the sources you have used if, for example, you have researched information in books or on the internet, or used particular sources as your inspiration. For each source, you should give the title and the original author's name. For a website, give the title and web address.

How should I write?

You should write in a style that allows a reader clearly to follow the information you are giving or the opinion you are putting forward.

> **Study tips**
>
> 1 Each sentence should make one important point.
> 2 You won't need many descriptive words (adjectives and adverbs) in this piece of writing because you need to concentrate on facts and keep your purpose clear.

Assignment 2: the expressive piece

You must write an expressive piece: descriptive and/or narrative.

What should I write?

The great thing about the expressive piece is that, provided you remember the key words **descriptive** and **narrative**, and make sure your piece matches at least one of these descriptions really well, you can choose any theme you like! Still, it's not always easy to come up with an idea that works, or to choose between different ideas that occur to you. Here are a few examples of ideas which would work well:

- a story involving a place you remember from when you were younger
- a story about a particular episode in your life which has had an impact on you (e.g. an accident or illness)
- a piece about family relationships and their importance
- a piece about friendships, perhaps when a person has proved themselves to be a friend – or has not!
- a science fiction story.

How should I write?

This second piece of writing should be written in a very different style from the first. Here there are no constraints. You can let your imagination take off. Use all the descriptive words and imagery, similes and metaphors, that you like. You don't have to write a series of points but can make your writing really vivid. You can experiment with using sentences of very different lengths, for instance. A journal or diary version of one of the ideas listed above might be one way to structure your writing.

AN UNCOMFORTABLE BED

Guy de Maupassant

One autumn I went to stay for the hunting season with some friends in a chateau in Picardy.

My friends were fond of practical joking, as all my friends are. I do not care to know any other sort of people.

When I arrived, they gave me a princely reception, which at once aroused distrust in my breast. We had some capital shooting. They embraced me, they cajoled me, as if they expected to have great fun at my expense.

I said to myself:

'Look out, old ferret! They have something in preparation for you.'

During the dinner, the mirth was excessive, far too great, in fact. I thought: 'Here are people who take a double share of amusement, and apparently without reason. They must be looking out in their own minds for some good bit of fun. Assuredly I am to be the victim of the joke. Attention!'

During the entire evening, everyone laughed in an exaggerated fashion. I smelled a practical joke in the air, as a dog smells game. But what was it? I was watchful, restless. I did not let a word or a meaning or a gesture escape me. Everyone seemed to me an object of suspicion, and I even looked distrustfully at the faces of the servants.

The hour rang for going to bed, and the whole household came to escort me to my room. Why? They called to me: 'Good night.' I entered the apartment, shut the door, and remained standing, without moving a single step, holding the wax candle in my hand.

I heard laughter and whispering in the corridor. Without doubt they were spying on me. I cast a glance around the walls, the furniture, the ceiling, the hangings, the floor. I saw nothing to justify suspicion. I heard persons moving about outside my door. I had no doubt they were looking through the keyhole.

An idea came into my head: 'My candle may suddenly go out, and leave me in darkness.'

Then I went across to the mantelpiece, and lighted all the wax candles that were on it. After that, I cast another glance around me without discovering anything. I advanced with short steps, carefully examining the apartment. Nothing. I inspected every article one after the other. Still nothing. I went over to the window. The shutters, large wooden shutters, were open. I shut them with great care, and then drew the curtains, enormous velvet curtains, and I placed a chair in front of them, so as to have nothing to fear from without.

Then I cautiously sat down. The armchair was solid. I did not venture to get into the bed. However, time was flying; and I ended by coming to the conclusion that I was ridiculous. If they were spying on me, as I supposed, they must, while waiting for the success of the joke they had been preparing for me, have been laughing enormously at my terror. So I made up my mind to go to bed. But the bed was particularly suspicious-looking. I pulled at the curtains. They seemed to be secure. All the same, there was danger. I was going perhaps to receive a cold shower-bath from overhead, or perhaps, the moment I stretched myself out, to find myself sinking under the floor with my mattress. I searched in my memory for all the practical jokes of which I ever had experience. And I did not want to be caught. Ah! Certainly not!

▶▶

Certainly not! Then I suddenly bethought myself of a precaution which I consider one of extreme efficacy: I caught hold of the side of the mattress gingerly, and very slowly drew it toward me. It came away, followed by the sheet and the rest of the bedclothes. I dragged all these objects into the very middle of the room, facing the entrance door. I made my bed over again as best I could at some distance from the suspected bedstead and the corner which had filled me with such anxiety. Then, I extinguished all the candles, and, groping my way, I slipped under the bedclothes.

For at least another hour, I remained awake, starting at the slightest sound. Everything seemed quiet in the chateau. I fell asleep.

I must have been in a deep sleep for a long time, but all of a sudden, I was awakened with a start by the fall of a heavy body tumbling right on top of my own body, and, at the same time, I received on my face, on my neck, and on my chest a burning liquid which made me utter a howl of pain. And a dreadful noise, as if a sideboard laden with plates and dishes had fallen down, penetrated my ears.

I felt myself suffocating under the weight that was crushing me and preventing me from moving. I stretched out my hand to find out what was the nature of this object. I felt a face, a nose, and whiskers. Then with all my strength I launched out a blow over this face. But I immediately received a hail of cuffings which made me jump straight out of the soaked sheets, and rush in my nightshirt into the corridor, the door of which I found open.

O stupor! It was broad daylight. The noise brought my friends hurrying into the apartment, and we found, sprawling over my improvised bed, the dismayed valet, who, while bringing me my morning cup of tea, had tripped over this obstacle in the middle of the floor, and fallen on his stomach, spilling, in spite of himself, my breakfast over my face.

The precautions I had taken in closing the shutters and going to sleep in the middle of the room had only brought about the interlude I had been striving to avoid.

Ah! How they all laughed that day!

This story, by one of the masters of short story writing, is an excellent example of the genre. It is short but it very cleverly does all the things that a short story needs to do. It has a number of the features of a short story which you might want to imitate.

- It has a good opening which leads you to want to read on as questions are left hanging: what practical joke will the narrator suffer at the hands of his friends? Will there, in fact, be any joke played on him?
- It develops the situation effectively through direct recounting of the narrator's thoughts, 'I was watchful, restless. I did not let a word or a meaning or a gesture escape me.', 'I was going perhaps to receive a cold shower-bath from overhead'.
- It leaves us wondering what the outcome will be, right up to the very end of the story. However, even at this point we are still left wondering if there is more to come and, now that the narrator is feeling secure, whether his friends will finally play the practical joke which he thinks he has avoided.

When writing your own stories, pay special attention to the beginning and the end, and think about every word and phrase. Ask yourself if it is the best word or phrase you can use. Don't always be content with your first ideas.

Study tips

You can approach the process of drafting and redrafting in a variety of ways; remember that redrafting does not mean just writing something out again and correcting any technical errors that were in the first effort.

1 You might ask your teacher to read the first version and suggest whether any parts could be improved. You could ask a friend or classmate to do the same. They might notice, for instance, that in a story you have created one character rather more strongly than another, and you might consider trying to give the second character more life. In an argumentative piece, you might have presented one side of the argument very much more strongly than the other, and you should try to balance them a bit more. Don't expect your teacher or friend to tell you **exactly** how to change your piece – it is, after all, your work and the final decision is up to you.
2 Try reading through the piece, asking yourself over and over again, 'Is this sentence necessary and is it as good as I can make it?'

Assignment 3: writing in response to text(s)

For this assignment you will need to write in response to a text or texts chosen by your Centre. This allows you, in consultation with your teacher, to find material on a topic in which you are particularly interested.

There are no specific limitations as to the sort of material you choose to write about (some possible examples are given later in this section), but your writing should meet the requirements either to analyse, review, comment or to argue, persuade, advise. You will be expected to choose passages which will allow you to select, analyse and evaluate facts, opinions and arguments.

The choice of passages is the responsibility of the Centre and you, as the student. You will also have the choice of how to present your response to the material. As long as you keep the purpose for which you are writing clearly in mind, you can choose to pursue it in any suitable format or genre which is appropriate.

Remember: for this assignment only, you will be assessed both for your **writing** and for your **reading** skills which will show how well you have responded to ideas in the text(s) you have chosen to write about.

What type of text(s) can I use?

You have a wide choice as to what texts you choose and where they come from. However, it is likely that non-fiction and media material will best suit the requirements of the syllabus. You should make sure that whatever text(s) you choose are of adequate length to contain sufficient ideas and details to allow you to respond to them as fully as you can. In this assignment it is your response to the **ideas** in the text(s) which is important.

Here are some suggestions of the type of material which could be used:

- advertisements and propaganda material
- newspaper and magazine articles and reports
- the words of speeches
- leaflets (such as those issued for charitable appeals)
- websites
- travel guides, travel brochures and literary travel writing
- the moving image. You may want to demonstrate how the use of moving pictures and other media devices helps to convey ideas but remember you must base your

writing on **reading** material and so you will need to provide a transcript of any film or television programme.

- literary material. You may use extracts from novels, plays, literary non-fiction or whole poems but whatever you choose must contain facts, opinions and/or arguments.

Remember: a copy of any material you use must be included in your coursework portfolio before it is sent for moderation.

How should I present my writing?

You have the opportunity to present your writing in any form which is appropriate. Whatever format you choose to use, however, you should think carefully about the audience for whom you are writing and the tone and register of what you write. Here are a few suggestions:

- an advertisement or series of advertisements for a particular product, accompanied by an explanation of the techniques and devices you have chosen to use in them and of how they are intended to appeal to their target audience
- your own newspaper article(s); letters to a newspaper giving opposing views about the material you have chosen to respond to
- the words of a speech you would give either supporting or opposing the ideas in your source material
- a leaflet dealing with issues similar to those in your source material and aimed to appeal to a particular audience
- your own travel guide/brochure written about an area you have visited or know well (however, it must be related to the original in a recognisable way)
- the script of a radio discussion between two or three people responding to the ideas and opinions in your source material
- a straightforward piece comparing the ideas and opinions in your source material and considering the methods used to communicate them to the chosen audience.

Warnings

1 **Check work done on a computer.** You are allowed to use a computer to produce your coursework and many people do. There are, however, a few things to remember. A computer is not the answer to all your linguistic problems. To use the spellcheck effectively, for example, you have to have a clear idea of the word that you want. It is amazing how many students scan the list of possibilities and pick the wrong word, so that what they end up with is nonsense. The same applies to the grammar check. Computer checks are not a substitute for your own knowledge.

2 **Don't copy!** We all read things that influence us and, if the model that influences us is good, it can have a positive effect. However, copying sections of other people's writing is called *plagiarism* and it is a form of cheating. Your teacher knows what your own writing is like and will immediately question work that is very different. In the same way, although you are encouraged to write in different styles, a moderator will be able to see quite easily if something does not belong to you. Cheats are nearly always caught out. If you have used ideas from books or the internet, remember to list your sources.

This remainder of this chapter provides a range of examples of coursework for Assignments 1 and 2 for you to read through. The teacher's annotations and comments are printed in red, and the teacher's overall analysis is printed in blue. The analysis of each piece includes an indication of the band that the work would be likely to achieve, so that you can see how the different strengths and weaknesses in the writing can have an effect on the marks.

At the end of the chapter you will find some examples of the sort of reading material that could be used as a basis for Assignment 3 and some suggestions for the sorts of tasks that could develop from it.

In the coursework samples that follow, there are examples of:

- informative/persuasive writing
- autobiographical writing
- short stories
- diary writing
- a package of items related to the process of getting a job.

As you make a start on your own coursework, consider these along with all the other ideas that have been mentioned and decide on your own way forward.

Examples of students' work for Assignment 1

Here are some examples of students' **informative, analytical and/or argumentative writing** for Assignment 1. They are written in different formats and aimed at different audiences but all fulfil the syllabus requirements of writing to inform, analyse or argue.

When producing work for this assignment it is important to keep the following points in mind:

- It is not necessary that any one piece of writing contains all three elements (inform, analyse and argue). However, you must ensure that what you write focuses clearly on one or two of them and that you use a tone that is fully appropriate to the type of writing you are producing. For example, when you are writing to inform, your tone is likely to be objective and impersonal, but if you are writing to argue, your tone may be more persuasive.
- It is important that you research information that you will use as a basis for what you write, but to score high marks you should ensure that you gain a clear understanding of the material you have researched so that what you write becomes personal to you and is not merely a summary of other people's ideas.

Here are two suggested tasks that may help you to start thinking.

- Produce a guide to your local area for people who may wish to visit it (*inform*). Say why it would be particularly suitable (or unsuitable) for young people of your age (*analyse*).
- Write a speech to your year group in which you try to persuade them for or against the view that in the future we will all be slaves to things like iPads and smartphones (*argue*).

Example 1

Water Safety

Ladies and Gentlemen, have you ever wondered about the dangers of swimming? As we all know, a swimming pool is a classic source of rest and relaxation during a hot day. A pool can also be a prime source of danger. Many children drown while swimming every year. A child's risk of drowning is much greater than most people like to think. Some amazing statistics show that children under the age of five are fourteen times as likely to die while in a pool than in a motor vehicle. To me that figure is absolutely astonishing and these deaths must be prevented. Children are not the only ones that fall victim to the pool, anyone can have accidents in and around the pool.

▶▶

Style

If you are in a swimming pool, do not let children run around the pool edge or they could slip over and fall causing severe injuries to themselves or others. It is dangerous to jump into the pool. Check first that there are no swimmers in the area. It is a dangerous act to duck and dunk people in the pool because it can destroy their confidence as a swimmer. Think about the other swimmers and try not to collide with them. If you do not look where you are going, especially if you are using equipment, you can hurt someone.

If your children are in or around the pool, someone needs to be watching them at all times. You can never ensure that no one will need assistance or help while in the pool but you can take the responsibility and the proper precautions to assure that if someone does need assistance, they are able to receive help rapidly and efficiently. Some of these precautions are as follows: place a fence around the pool, or cover the top of the pool when it is not in use. This has reduced the risk of drowning by 70 per cent in some areas around the world. You as the responsible adult must remain vigilant by constantly watching your children while they are in the pool. Most deaths are due to the fact that the children panic and as they try to yell for help, water is swallowed and as they try to cough up the water, they swallow more. As a result they are not able to be heard and will sadly drown. According to past personal experience, children can not be left alone even for you, as the adult, to go and answer the door. Anyone taking care of children that are in the water should know Cardiopulmonary Resuscitation or CPR and should be prepared to use it in an emergency.

We must learn to become our own lifesavers and should always prepare for emergencies. For example, mark the pool's deep end; place a circular buoy on a rope, a long handled hook and a rescue ladder at the poolside. You should also have a poolside telephone with emergency phone numbers posted next to it because it is both a convenience and a critical safety feature.

Some essentials that you need to know are getting into the water when the depth is unknown and while wearing clothing, how to undress and remove heavy articles of clothing while keeping the light ones on, and know how to swim or float in clothing. A few more precautions that should be taken are to teach your children not to panic when they are in and around the pool. They should know when to yell for help, and to be patient and cooperate to the person trying to help them. Teach them how to stay erect with their head clearly above the water.

Say you see a person yelling for help, do you think it is safe for you to jump into the water to save them? In these situations, you cannot follow your instincts and instead, you must use your head. If you jump in after someone, it could result with both of you in extreme trouble. This is because of the panic factor. Every human being, when in trouble, start panicking. When people panic, they can not control their actions and two out of three end up hurting the person that is trying to save them. If it is possible to reach the person from the side of the pool, do it. Find anything, like a plank or a beach ball, which could be used as a floatation device. Give help by voice and tell the person who needs help to keep his/her arms under the water and not to struggle. Stay aware of the situation all the time because statistics show that many people drown within ten metres of safety. Helping someone calm down may save a life.

It is impeccable that the safety precautions that were explained are not only taken notice of but they must be put into action as well. This information has not been given to you to scare you, but on the contrary, it has been given to you to ensure that your time in the pool is made more fun because now you know that you and your children are safe.

Teacher's analysis: This informative piece of writing states clearly situations which can exist around and in a swimming pool. The tone is good in that it remains serious and clear. However, the material is not as well ordered as it might be and is a little repetitive. There are also errors of expression and the occasional clumsiness, and some misspelling.

Example 2

This piece consisted of four items related to a successful job application: the job advert (below), the letter of application and CV (below and on page 132), a reference letter (page 132) and a letter from the student to a friend (page 133).

SECRETARY REQUIRED FOR RELIANCE AGENCIES

Responsibilities: Answering phone calls, typing documents, emailing, booking meetings, computing and other basic secretarial skills.

Necessary Qualifications: A typing speed of 90 words per minute, and a shorthand speed of 110 words per minute. Familiarity with an Apple Mac computer system would be an advantage.

Terms of Appointment: A salary of K2000 per month (excluding bonus), working days Mon–Fri, 8.30am to 6.30pm. One month paid holiday. A company car will be provided. Benefits include a sickness scheme and insurance. You will be trained on an upgrading scheme while you are in the job. You will be working in a modern spacious office.

Closing date for receipt of completed applications is 18 May 2013.

For further details and application form, please write to Mr Peter Green, Appointments Officer, Chayamba Building, PO Box 123, Lilongwe. Tel: 654 321 123 456.

PO Box 277
Lilongwe
Malawi
Telephone: 987654

19 April 2013

Appointment's Officer
Chayamba building
PO Box 123
Lilongwe Malawi

Dear Mr Green,

I would like to apply for the post of secretary, which I saw advertised in the 'Daily Times' on 18 April 2013.

I am a single, but intend to get married in two years. I am 22 years old. I have a typing speed of 50 words per minute, and a shorthand speed of 110 words per minute. I have passed 8 GCSEs and 3 A Levals. I have my own Apple Mac, and fully know how to operate it.

I am applying for this job as I wanted a higher salary, than my previous job. Also your office is idealy situated for me as I live 3 minutes away from Chayamba building.

I have worked at ICI for 3 years and enclose a referance from the Manager and from my headmaster.

Yours sincerly,

S------- T--------

CV

Name: S------- T--------

Address: PO Box 277, Lilongwe, Malawi

Telephone number: 987654

Date of Birth: 14 February 1991

Nationality: British Citizen

School's Attended: Central Secondary School, Speed typing school Lilongwe, Shorthand School Lilongwe

Exam Results: (GCSE) 4 A's, 3 B's, 1 C (A Level) 3 B's, typing school certificate: 50 word's per minute, shorthand certificate: 110 words per minute.

Experience: Further on the job training for 3 years with IBM, Blantyre. Office Secretary at ICE for 3 years

References: Headmaster of school, Manager of ICI

The Headmaster
Central School
P.B. 999
Lilongwe

20 April 2013

Appointments Officer
Chayamba Building
PO Box 123
Lilongwe

Dear Mr Peter Green

This is a letter of Reference to S------- T--------, who has applied for the job of a secretary.

S------- has achieved high grades in his exams, and has done well in his academic school career. Although at times his standards did drop; he just needed a push to come back up again. When he first came to the school, he did not display a mature and sensible approach towards his studies. However, after his seven year stay at Central, he has developed a serious attitude, and shows promising performance in the future.

When it came to sports, S------- was not too keen, but later on he did participate in team sports such as tennis and cricket. Although he did not exeed on the field, S------- won several awards on weight lifting.

S------- is a polite and well manerred boy.

I have enclosed his last Report and period work order book.

Yours sincerly

A.B.Davies

PO Box 277
Lilongwe
Malawi
Telephone: 987654
Office: 456789
3 June 2013

Dear Mark,

Yo! Mark, you know that job you told me to apply for? Well thats what I did, and guess what? I got it! The company first changed my place, so I'm going to be moving into the new house soon. They are still trying to organise a car for me. I should be coming over to South Africa soon for a month's paid holiday.

Anyway when I first went to work, I met this really friendly man. He showed me my office, and how to operate the office phone and email systems. I have one of those phones where I just transfer the call to whoever the caller wants, it's like a switchboard. When I received my first caller for the Manager, by mistake I sent it to the general manager but still they weren't too angry about it, because they know I'm new. Every half an hour this man comes from all the offices to give me letters to typ, or put on the computor, so I try to do all that in half an hour before the next lot come's in. It's difficult so I asked him to come every 45 minitus. If I still can't finish it. I take it home. At the Lunch Break, everyone was asking me how I was getting on. After lunch 2.00pm to 3.00pm I get a special training course. After this I carry on with the usual routine. I finish the work and go home.

They really work hard here!
your mate,

S-------

Teacher's analysis: The work is well structured and there is enough content to fit it for its purpose. There is variety of style. Spelling is not good: 'levals', 'referance', 'sincerly', 'computor'. Maybe this task would not easily show evidence to justify a band 1, but it is confident enough for **band 4/3** despite the errors.

Example 3

Animal Vivisection: A Cruel Science.

Animal Vivisection is an under-publicised, yet widespread problem about which something must be done. I will begin with the UCLA's 'spinal research centre' in California. I ask you to imagine yourself as a fifteen-month-old cat; you are in an underground lab along with hundreds of other cats. Your back has been crushed violently by lead weights, your entire body has been shaven, and electrodes have been implanted in your head and tail. You have just been subjected to twin blasts of hot air to your face and electric shocks to your paws and tail. You are in for 119 more before you are finally put out of your misery, if you don't die from the electric torture first.

This is called the 'fear test'; the electrodes monitor a current passed trough the cats' spines and monitor the response from the brain and change in heart rate throughout the experiment. These experiments have been going on for many years now and yet there is still no evidence that they have any connection with treating human back pains.

Other examples of this torture are in uncounted labs across the world where cruel and heartless experiments are being carried out by doctors on rats, dogs, cat, rabbits and even our closest relatives in the animal kingdom; monkeys. For the rats there is 'the maze'; an experiment where a rat is placed in a maze at the end of which are two doors, behind one, a piece of cheese, behind the other, a wire giving an electric shock. You can imagine the results when the rat finds the wire. This is bad enough, but what happens then the doors are switched? Or when there is a shock behind both doors? The poor rats are eventually driven mad, or die from shock. Dogs and cats have medical drugs tested on them, sometimes resulting in great sickness or even death. This experiment is pointless anyway as dogs and cats have differing reactions to that of humans regarding medicines. An example of this is the drug Paracetamol which has healing properties to humans but is lethal to dogs! Monkeys are being subjected to tests in relation to smoking, usually developing lung cancer, or tar lined lungs, eventually killing them. The saddest thing about these experiments is that most of them go unpublished, so even if the results were relevant, they are never released to the public, so the same experiments are repeated over and over again. ✓

In the cosmetic world, make-up is tested on animals such as pigs and rabbits. Make-up found to be corrosive usually dissolves an animal's face before they are removed. Hairspray is sprayed up Rabbits' noses to find out if it is harmful to the sinuses; those that are usually result in sneezing, causing convulsions so great that they break the animal's back.

My request to those reading this article is this: Please think on these examples of cruelty to animals, and the pointlessness of most of them, the very fact that we are a different species to those we are testing OUR products on, and take action to ban Vivisection world-wide. A positive example of people taking action to halt the pain caused on animals is the banning of the sale of fur taken from slaughtered animals, and if we just follow this example, and remember that it was on the request of everyday people that brought about this banning, we can bring the cruelty of Animal Vivisection to an end. ✓

Teacher's comment: Low band 1 Well argued! A powerful catalogue of examples to shock the reader!

Teacher's analysis: This is a piece of informative/argumentative writing in which the student tries effectively to persuade the reader to share his views. It is clearly a subject about which the student feels strongly and he writes well and remains focused on his argument. There are occasional typing errors which ought to have been corrected.

Examples of students' work for Assignment 2

Here are some examples of students' **descriptive and/or narrative writing** for Assignment 2.

Example 1

SURVIVING VICTIM

The Galactic Empire was falling.

It was a colossal Empire, stretching across millions of worlds, millions of light years apart. Its fall was colossal too – and a long one, as Hari Seldon had predicted …

The memories were fragmentary at first, as they always were … He had been walking the dirty, scorched streets in silence since twilight first began to gather. His steps were steady and monotonous. Pain streamed like liquid fire through every cell of his body – but he locked it away in a corner of his mind, ignored it and walked. It was all a shock to him. All was new. All was horrific.

Dim soft sunlight barely reached the soft black soil beneath his silent steps. Its rays were blocked by fine glittering dust like mist on a humid day, only it wasn't. There was little, In fact nothing to please the eye in his surroundings. In fact, it was the exact opposite. He looked to the falling dust in hatred and screamed, '*Who* and *why*?' only it was as silent as his dead surroundings. Questions upon questions, mysteries upon mysteries heaped themselves up in his mind, with this question plaguing him as fiercely as the pain.

He continued, threading his way through the clatter and glitter of the streets, thronged with shrivelled corpses clustered around the tawdry attractions offered to space-weary visitors – everything from ordinary holoscreens to shadowy, semi-illicit drug dives. Vegetation was grudgingly available, or what was left of it. Trees were left bare and naked in the dim light as if to say 'come what may come,' only it already came.

Broken, fleeting visions of landscape passed his mind as he had seen them from his spaceship – a bleak inhospitable world, dominated by chill expanses of desert, by towering ranges of rock-fanged mountains. His name was Elijah Bailey. It was his world – the planet Aurora. It had had breathable air, with water, and vegetation sprawled all over its surface. it also had had a variety of its own life forms – the venomous reptiles of many weird shapes, the deadly jungle cats, the huge, horned mammoths of the mountains, the tangled vine growths that fed on flesh – all alien beasts, all threatening, all dangerously elegant. Now, this was non-existent. It was now a dead and deadly world.

His memories were gathering pace now, and Elijah writhed in his chair, powerless to stop his unconscious mind from forming images that he had re-lived so often before, in horror and despair. Elijah Bailey's memories shifted back, as they always did, and the broken, fleeting visions gathered, held steady …

As he studied the face of the planet Aurora looming and filling his view-screen, all seemed puzzlingly calm and normal. There was a faint, hazy aura round the image of the planet and the spaceship's sensors reported unknown radiation, but Elijah discounted that as a possible minor malfunction of the screen and the sensors, to do with the lack of repairs that resulted from the lack of funds the falling Empire suffered from. The planet had been attacked and unknown radiation released over the entire surface. The planet was bathed in a glowing haze of lethal radiation, in which everything and everyone that Elijah had loved had met their deaths.

►►

Now, Elijah's face twisted, his body hunched, aching, torn with a fury that was beyond bearing, a grief that was inconsolable, and a physical sensation – pain. It seemed to emanate from his very bones – faint, but tangible and definite. A deep-lying sensation of burning pain. Horror and savage rage tore at his sanity. But in the end as the hours passed, something else – not intuition but a physical sensation itself, from within his body – told him that even though he had survived, it was not likely to matter to him for very long. He was to meet with his fellow victims of the falling Empire soon. He was to meet them in nowhere but heaven – he was dying a slow and painful death ...

The medic had made exhaustive tests. And the gloom that appeared on his face was enough to tell Elijah the results. The radiation – from some altered isotope unrecognised by either Elijah or the medic – had reached Elijah despite his wearing a radiation-proof suit and settled in Elijah's bones. There it was creating cellular changes and breakdowns that were surely, inevitably, killing him now.

'A month more.' Elijah remembered the space medic saying, 'Two at the most.'

Time was now his most precious possession. Every minute gone was another step towards the day – soon now as the medic had said – when the pain would grow strong enough to batter down his control, when the radiation within him would overwhelm and quench his life.

Elijah began looking forward to the end – not only as a release from the pain. It would also release him from the memories that came to torment his nights, in which he relived the terrible day when he thought he was rushing to visit his planet and found he had come to join it only in death.

And it would release him from the despair which came with the growing realisation that the Galactic Empire was certainly falling. Hari Seldon's prediction was no joke. But afterall, who would think that such a powerful empire would disintegrate to rubble.

The flavour of that anticipation reached into the memory, filled it, changed it. For the first time in weeks, the surviving victim of the Empire's fall sank deeper into peaceful, undisturbed sleep, moving closer and closer towards his fate.

The fact was inescapable. It was that many more wars were happening, everywhere, than should have been happening. Entire solar systems were erupting with violence. A large industrialised planet would move suddenly and inexplicably attack a smaller, under-developed neighbour. Alternatively, two small planets came to invade – without clear cause – a third, and then after their victory fall out and fight between themselves. Elijah had witnessed it right before his very eyes. Hari Seldon had foreseen it.

The Galactic Empire was falling. Its people had to *accept* it, as a religion is accepted. No sane human could deny it.

Teacher's comment: Band 1 *An effective short story – well written and making effective use of description. The student captures and sustains the genre. Well done!*

Teacher's analysis: *There are some delightful phrases in the piece of imaginative writing which is a sophisticated piece of science fiction writing. We could pick out so many but here is just one: 'the venomous reptiles of many weird shapes'. What is perhaps surprising is that the note at the beginning says that it is a first draft. Normally a second draft might have improved the vocabulary and one or two of the ideas might be reworked but there is no necessity for that here. This student understands science fiction writing and can employ exactly the right tone.*

Example 2

The Englishman

Having spent the last six weeks of my life in these desolate trenches I feel that telling this story is my last stab at sanity after the suicidal attack on the German trench that has been the major focus of the last six weeks of my life.

I am Edward Molden, a soldier in the 3rd regiment of King George V's army, stationed on the French frontline. It is 1917 and we have been at war with the Hun for three years now. I was drafted last year and was transferred here six weeks ago, and the strange thing is that I still have no idea where I am, only that it is the north of France; I have heard mention that we are near Ypres, but no one is sure anymore. In the regiment to which I am assigned I have one friend with whom I am close, name Robert Paulson, or Bob for short. He and I have been together since basic training and I feel that he is the only one in this regiment who I believe I could trust my life to in this slow-moving, pointless war.

I will begin my story when Bob and I were transferred to this area of, I think, Ypres in which we are now stationed. My first view of the area was one of grim desolation; trees stripped bare by the impacts of shelling; land trodden underfoot, brown and muddy with quagmires littering the area of no-mans land that lay between us and the German trench; and the vast stretches of barbed wire, coiled around rotting corpses and bones, which were picked clean by rats, stretched as far as I could see. The damp, cold wind whipped my face and I could already smell death in the air. I saw what was left of the regiment we were replacing, the 5th I think, ambling, some limping, away from the trenches, coughing, cursing the Kaiser, the King and even God for bringing them to this terrible place. As we stepped off the train, behind me Bob mumbled something or other and I turned and faced him. He was almost as tall as me, with azure-blue eyes and short, black hair. He was a very handsome man, and I think before the war he had married a woman and had a child.

'God Eddy, look at this damn place! It's like a little slice of hell, right here on earth,' he said, frowning, 'and have you seen the troops we're replacing?' He shook his head; 'They're broken men.'

I gazed out across the shell-shocked, the crippled, the maimed and felt for the first time, a deep sense of foreboding about this place.

We were quickly marched into the trenches, re-briefed on the "Don'ts" of trench warfare: don't stick your head above the parapet; when on nightwatch don't light a cigarette; don't ever retreat until the order is given; and all the other orders we had heard a thousand times before. Soon we were off and setting up our sleeping quarters.

About four days after our arrival at the trenches, we experienced a gas attack and, although I remained unhurt, we lost four men, so replacements from other regiments were transferred to ours. On of the men transferred to our regiment was and Irishman named Patrick O'Flannery, a charismatic man; not the brightest I've known, but a good man, and some one who I got along with very well. He was of medium height with short, curly hair, and was well built. The most memorable thing about him was his strong Cork accent, which was mocked furiously by the rest of the regiment but I found very endearing. Bob found his optimism towards life refreshing and was always laughing about the fact that he never stopped talking about 'after the war'.

It was about ten days after the arrival of the Irish troops and the rain had set in. The rain has always made me miserable and this was no exception. I thought of home, my friends who I has left behind, my house in Dorset and then remembered where I was; in some muddy trench, probably getting trench-foot in these cheap leather boots I was wearing, all around me people dying for a cause no-one cared about anymore. ►►

We had been given the order to attack the German trench by the start of next week and were all busy preparing for the attack. In the days leading up to our charge on the Germans, there wasn't one of us who wasn't quaking in his boots at the thought of running out into the German machine-gunners' firing line. Over this time Patrick and I had become better friends and had constant conversations about everything. On the second day before the attack we were having one such conversation after Patrick had returned from the gun post:

'I tell ya Ed, I was looking t'rew that periscope over there, and I haven't seen that much dirt in all me life! It's like a nightmare, all them dead men, just rotting there, it ain't right!'

'I wonder how many,' Interrupted Bob.

'How many what?' I asked.

'How many have died so far?'

'It most be at least t'ree million,' guessed Patrick, 'But as long as I ain't one of them, it don't matter to me.'

'I tell you something though,' started Bob, 'I'm bloody worried about Monday; the attack'll be pure suicide; they've got machine guns you know.'

'Yeah but as long as God's on our side, we'll get t'rough!'

Proclaimed Patrick, as optimistic as ever, and walked off to get some food from the mess.

Poor lad, I thought, doesn't know what he's in for .

This was it. Monday. The day we had all been dreading. As I stood waiting for the Sergeant to blow his whistle, thoughts of home raced through my mind: Would I make it out alive? What would happen to my friends? Would we be victorious? Before I could consider the outcome of these worries I heard the deafening whistle for attack and before I realised what was happening I was over the parapet, screaming at the top of my lungs and charging towards the Hun. I saw a spray of bullets come out of the German trench and watched five of my allies drop to the ground in agony, clutching their chests as they fell. To my right were Bob and Patrick, both making good ground, dodging machine gun fire and various explosions. Patrick was making particularly good ground and was almost on top of a machine gun post, with a grenade in his hand as he approached the panicking German. He raised his arm, threw the grenade, blowing up the post and gunner. Just as he began to slow his pace and dodge another blast of machine gun fire, he disappeared in a flash of smoke and an almighty bang. He had stepped on a landmine and been blown apart right before my eyes. I slowed to a stop and, frozen with horror, stood motionless trying to make sense of what had just happened.

I suddenly felt a powerful jarring of my shoulder and the world became a blur as I slammed into the wet, muddy ground with a thud. When I regained vision I saw Bob's familiar face, looking panicked with a stream of bullets whizzing above his head. He had seen me get shot and rushed to my aid, dragging me into the shell hole in which we were now hiding.

'We've gotta get out of here Ed!' he said in a frantic tone, 'The Hun's killed most of the regiment and they're still shooting at us! I think we'll have to wait until it's dark and then crawled back , ok?'

I mumbled some attempt at recognition and threw up, the pain in my shoulder making me sick. I felt my eyes becoming heavy and then lost consciousness.

All I can remember of the four or so hours in which we took getting back to the trench, dodging sniper fire and hiding in shell holes, was a deep sense of gratitude that I felt for Bob, who was carrying me back to the trench on his back. When I came to I was lying on my back in a stretcher in this trench with Bob by my side.

'The train I'll be here in a couple of hours,' started Bob, 'then you should be ok. I heard talk that the Hun was badly hit during the attack and they're launching a counter? offensive, with the 9th regiment, he continued, his face suddenly looking very worried again, 'and me; along what's left of this one …'

Lovely! Well done!
with

Example 3

Zoo Story

Synopsis

Mr. Moni, the head keeper of a small zoo in Zimbabwe, is a tall, old, and always grumpy man. He has been the keeper of the zoo for about 25 years, as long as any of the animals can remember. He also has a unsettled homelife and is often in an angry mood after having a row with his wife. After these arguments he takes his anger out on the animals by mistreating them and because of this all of the animals hate him. He loves to terrorize the animals and he likes to pick on one in particular every night. Her name was Jennifer and she is a ten-year-old chimpanzee with extreme intelligence. Jennifer is liked by all that see her because she the famous monkey who has been taught to eat with a fork and knife.

After two weeks of observing the actions of Mr. Moni, Jennifer formulated a plan to rid the entire animals of human oppression forever. She called a meeting of all of the animals and explained he plan to them. They were all excited to rid themselves of the humans they hated so much and were anxious to get the plan underway. The plan was every night a different animal would take turns distracting Mr. Moni while Jennifer used the one tool that had access to, her knife, to cut the bars of her cage. Their plan worked well because of Mr. Moni's reliability.

After two weeks of this every night, Jennifer finished her work. She, Alex and Suhail escaped from their cage and freed the bear, the lion and the tiger so that they would be able to attack Mr. Moni. That night, it was Bijan, the parrot's turn to distract Mr. Moni. Mr. Moni however had a different idea and was desperately trying to hit Bijan with a tick he had acquired from a nearby tree. Jennifer and the others came up behind Mr. Moni without making a sound and attacked him before he knew what was going on. Finally, Claire, the bear, carried him behind some bushes and that is where Mr. Moni screamed his last scream.

Chapter 1

After the death of Mr. Moni, all the animals were freed and they all celebrated until Alex said, 'Friends, we still have one more minor problem. What about the other keeper, Mr. Salman? He starts work at seven.'

Then Jennifer said, 'Don't worry, we will be ready for him. I've got another plan.'

For the remainder of the night the animals assembled everything that they would need to destroy Mr. Salman. At seven o'clock the following morning, Mr. Salman entered the zoo. He started his usual rounds of the zoo when he realized that there was no animal in any of the cages. To his shock, he was the only one in sight. In a panic he began to run back to the office to call Mr. Moni. Just as he turned the last corner before the office he skidded to a halt. He was frozen stiff. All of the animals were in front of him in a barricade. They all just stood there and stared at him. He saw the red in their eyes and could not move a muscle. Suhail swung to the gate and made absolutely certain that it was licked securely. Mr. Moni and Mr. Salman were hung on the outside of the gate as an example and a sign of the animals' new found independence.

▶▶

Jennifer, after much effort, quieted the group of animals and said, 'We have just taken a great step to the independence of this zoo and I am extemely proud of each and everyone of you, but, we still have one complication, Mr. Amin will be very upset.' ✓

Mr. Amin is the rich owner of the zoo. Jennifer continued, 'Soon he will be receiving a lot of questions and complaints about the status of the zoo. He will most definitely come to see what is going on in here. The problem is that it is impossible to tell when he will come or whom he will bring with him, so we must be prepared at all times. You might be asking yourself how we are going to eat and live but do not worry, Bijan has been sent to search for the storage room. There will be a truckload of food coming every month but Mr. Amin can not know about this. If he does, he will put a stop to it and we will starve.'

Chapter 2

Two weeks passed and the storage room was found. The animals did nothing but playing around and having fun. The animals were able to come and go to eat whenever they were wanted. Jennifer was extremely reserved as she stayed in her cage most of the time and she kept to herself. No one except Suhail understood Jennifer very well and this is how she liked to keep it. Suhail and Alex were spending a tremendous amount of time together.

One day, the two animals that were lookouts spotted Mr. Amin on his way to the zoo. They went and warned the rest of the animals. As Mr. Amin approached the gate, he spotted the two dead bodies, screamed and ran to his car. ✓

Three days later, the animals spotted him again but this time six vans, two police cars and a fire engine followed him into the parking lot. The vans had painting on the side that read 'ANIMAL CONTROL'. People were getting out of the vehicles with all kinds of weapons.

The animals saw them coming so they all decided to hide in the storage room. That way, they would have all of the food and water they would need for a long time. Most of the animals had never seen a gun before therefore they did not there was any reason to be scared. Jennifer's plan was to wait until Mr. Amin and others opened the storage door and the animals would attack them with all of their brute strength. The men arrived and they flung open the door, more the one hundred animals came running out of the door trampling half of the men. Some of the men turned and ran away while others stayed and began shooting.

During this tragic battle only 35 animals survived and half of the food was destroyed, along with most of the zoo. If there was a second attack on the zoo, the animals would not stand a chance against the attackers. The animal did not celebrate after their first great battle because of the deaths of their fellow animals, including Alex and Claire. ✓

Bijan was sent to other zoos around the country to inform them of their continued success. A few months past and Jennifer and Suhail spent more time together and fell in love. Everyone else <u>were</u> enjoying themselves immensely, just eating and sleeping. All of the animals new Mr. Amin would come back and that he would bring others with him so they were making the most of the time they had left.

This is the beginning of my story. The rest of the main events in the story are listed below. ✓

1   Two years past and Jennifer was the leader of the zoo.
2   There was a shortage of food so she decided to put rations.
3   The zoo got very dirty so the animals had to work and clean the place up.
4   Two months past and there was no electricity and there was not a lot of food left.
5   The other larger animals did not treat Bijan very well so he became very angry and decided to leave.
6   Bijan told the other zoos of their situation and that the animals will not last long.
7   Some other zoos started to help them and sent them some gifts like little scraps of food.

8   Now the animals in the zoo do not have food, electricity or any connection to other zoos.

9   Suhail and many other animals were getting old and were very sick. They knew they would not be able to survive another attack from Amin.

10 Suhail died and Jennifer lost all her hope and thought it was not worth living anymore.

11 Two weeks later Amin came in with an army of men. The animals, including Jennifer, ignored them and did not even try to fight. All the animals were caught. Some of them were slaughtered or sold. Jennifer was about to be sold to an English family but one day she was found dead.

12 Amin decided to reopen the zoo.

13 Two new monkeys were placed in Jennifer's cage and they saw a crossed out note carved in the wall. It was from Jennifer saying 'If anyone sees this, always remember not to give up and always have faith in yourself, even if there is not a big chance in achieving your goal. My goal was to become free from this zoo and I did not have a big chance but at the end, I achieved it.' √

Teacher's analysis: 'Zoo Story' works quite successfully, although it rather lacks substance in its middle section; we don't get much idea about how the animals live and the idea of a regular delivery of food continuing with Mr Amin not realising he is paying for it is not very successful. There are errors, although some of them may be the result of failing to proofread. A low **band 3/2**.

Example 4

This student chose to submit some original poetry for Assignment 2 and has closely followed the syllabus instructions by providing a commentary about how the poetry came to be written.

Planning Poem One

Most of my good poetry requires a bit of sitting back and relaxing, thinking long and hard about what I really want to say. As with most writing, one idea sparked another in my mental process. Originally, I had heard the quote, 'I have no proof that God does not exist, but I rather He not,' by an atheist. The very fact that this man said that he has no proof is saying that God does indeed exist! Here he is unwisely contradicting himself and in my opinion, making himself seem very ignorant. Thinking that there is no God does *not* mean He doesn't exist. A human can not control that. God is God and that's final no matter what humans have to say.

From this quote, I had the idea to use other quotes said by famous people in a poem *about* God. This was done through research on the internet. A man had set up a website about Albert Einstein. There were about fifty quotes that he had compiled that Einstein had made in his life. I copied the ones that I thought could be incorporated into a poem (see below).

Quotes Made By Albert Einstein

'God is subtle but he is not malicious.'

'The most beautiful thing we can experience is the mysterious. It is the source of all true art and science.'

'Nature to him was an open book, whose letters he could read without effort.'

'Nature hides her secrets because of her essential loftiness but not by means of ruse.'

'Science without religion is lame, religion without science is blind.'

'When I am judging a theory, I ask myself whether, if I were God, I would have arranged the world in such a way.'

Other Quotes that I Have Also Heard Before

'Faith is the evidence of things unseen.'

'I have no proof that God does not exist, but I rather He not.'

'Everything around us points to a higher wisdom.'

Quotes which I ended up using.

Getting Started on Poem One

It was unclear at the beginning of this poem which quotes I wanted to and would be able to use in the poem. First I tried out the quote of, 'I have no proof that God does not exist, but I rather He not.' Following are some ways I experimented with to incorporate it into the first verse.

This is what I wanted to say, but somehow intermix the quote within the verse.

She says there is no God
and yet she screams
and curses Him; demanding
to be heard.
The non-existent I thought
was said.
*I have no proof that God
does not exist – but I rather
He not.*

An attempt at inserting the quote, which didn't come out as clearly as first intended. Some words were also changed.

She says there is no God,
with no proof that He
does not exist; and yet she screams
and curses Him, demanding
to be heard. Rather He not
be, and so He isn't. The
non-existent I thought
was said.

This is the beginning of a slightly different version. I decided not to develop it further as I realised it wasn't going anywhere.

She says there is nothing,
having no proof that God
does not exist; screaming
and cursing Him; determined
to shut Him out

All of these variations didn't seem to quite 'connect' and smoothly flow into other verses. The second variation was the most likable, but in many ways seemed too wordy and confusing for the reader. When trying to use this as the starting of a poem, I wasn't able to get anywhere with it. None of my ideas for the other quotes followed the way I put the first verse. Therefore, I decided to make a fresh start and banish all of my first intents.

My God in Einstein's Words

Lost people
of this world; holding vague images
of an obscure being, watching
with an etched scowl, white hair
robe billowing as a cloudy dust bowl
up, up in the sky; a silent observer who
strikes with lighting bolts every
so often.
True, my **God is subtle** *— understated and*
misunderstood by man — **but He's not malicious**.

Small minds of humans, engrossed
in their favorite preoccupation: denying my God.
Rippling muscles, beating
bloody hearts, brains with complex turns
and twists all came from nothing
with nothing — **science without my God is lame**.
Locked away, not turning the key
of probing and exploring
to discover the wide
open doors — **religion without science is blind**.

Musty books, laced
with crinkly old smells, bug-eyed
fluorescent screens, lined with information,
and yet we have only made
a dent in this metallic ocean of unknown.
Nature hides her secrets
because of her essential loftiness, *the reminder*
of who the Creator is; not deceptively, but plainly
supreme.
Sound waves bouncing
back and forth; leaking out
of the atmosphere into space,
vigorously leaping further
and further to nameless places. Dying
stars, ticking human thoughts, sizzling
energy; brimming with the
mysteries of my God —
the most beautiful thing
we can experience.
*Words in **bold** *are quotes that Albert Einstein made in the course of his life.*

The parts that I used from some of Einstein's quotes are in bold. Some are changed or cut off a bit, but the original meaning is not lost.

Commentary on 'My God in Einstein's Words'

The length of this poem is deceiving as it is only one page long, but could easily have ten pages of explanation. 'My God in Einstein's Words' is all about God. On the surface, the poem has two characteristics. One is the spacing. I tried to imitate Margaret Atwood's style of spacing and use of punctuation, especially the semicolon. None of my previous poetry has included the semicolon. In some cases, I think that it is good to use it. It gives the right type of pause and flowing connection to certain parts of poetry. The second characteristic of this poem is that I included quotes from Albert Einstein. I incorporated parts of the quotes in certain areas. These quotes are what ultimately sparked and shaped my ideas.

Everything said in 'My God in Einstein's Words' is about *my* God. Whenever 'God' is mentioned in it, 'my' follows before. This is important as it means that I am not talking about somebody else's god, but mine. I do not have the universalistic view that all gods are the same one God.

To explain this poem, we must concentrate on what the quotes mean. In the first stanzas, the quote is, 'God is subtle, but He's not malicious.' This quote is used as a correction to what was said before it about God. People think very vaguely about God and see Him as a being up in the sky who looks down and punishes them. I used the image of 'robe billowing as a cloudy dust bowl' to describe part of it. It compares a dust bowl in a desert to the white robes of God that so often flash into people's minds. I used the semicolon twice in the stanza. I wanted a longer pause than a comma, but not a complete full stop. The semicolon connects the two parts together in the desired way.

The next quote was, 'Science without religion is lame, religion without science is blind.' I changed it a little bit as the poem is supposed to be *about* God, *not* religion. The two can be very different things. There is a comparison made in this stanza. While humans are always trying to deny that there is a God in science, they are forgetting that the very thoughts and brains that they are thinking with are from God, 'rippling muscles, beating bloody hearts, brains with complex turns and twists.' The 'b' sound is repeated here to make it sound as if the heart is actually pumping. 'All came from nothing with nothing,' is referring to the 'Big Bang Theory'. What is my view on this? 'Science without my God is lame.' The last part of the stanza goes on the reverse side. On the other hand, it is also wrong to turn a cold shoulder to science and the knowledge about our world it has to offer us. The next stanza explains this more fully. Books with 'crinkly old smells' and computers with 'bug-eyed fluorescent screens' have a huge amount of information that Science has explained. Every day, new things are being discovered. Science makes us realise that there is so much that we do not know. It is as if we have only made a small imprint in a sheet of metal, 'a dent in this metallic ocean of unknown.' As Einstein says, 'Nature hides her secrets because of essential loftiness.' In other words, nature is so complex because of the Creator (God). The complexity proves that there must be a higher wisdom behind all of it.

The last stanza is full of unusual, peculiar images. I used the image of sound waves seeping out of the earth's atmosphere to show the vastness of the universe, 'vigorously leaping further and further to nameless places.' Sound waves along with 'dying stars, ticking human thoughts, sizzling energy' are strange things that are happening all of the time without anybody paying attention to or thinking about them. If we were to sit back and think about these things, we would see God in all of them. This, as Einstein's quote says, is 'the most beautiful thing we can experience.'

Teacher's analysis: This piece [on pages 141–44] is very original. It is a clear account of how the student planned and wrote her own poem and a very competent explanation of some of the images within it. The piece of explanation at the end is not trying to write a formal poetry commentary but a personal analysis of how the poem was put together. The poem itself is beautifully constructed, using strong images and provoking lots of questions. It really is a very striking piece of work and would gain a **secure band** 1.

Example 5

Lost

√

Effective detail

I switched on the light. The bright light shone in all parts of the lab. Two other scientists were seated in the centre of the room.

'The robot,' they stated. 'Have you thought about it?'

√

'No,' I replied. 'What's there to think about anyway?'

The first scientist stood up, pushed his chair to one side and moved towards me. His mouth twitched in both corners of his lips.

'You clearly know that the robot will have to lose one sense.' He paused for a moment, then continued, 'Which will it be?'

I went on to speak, then '----.' There was a blank. My mind just blanked out. I sat down slowly whilst holding fast onto the corner of a chair. I had nothing to say. One sense had to be removed, but which? I sat back in the chair, trying to make myself as comfortable as possible.

'So …' one scientist groaned sarcastically.

My mouth turned dry. What could I do? I had to make a science project decision that could change the mind of the robot to do specific jobs. My eyes strained hard at the scientists. My eyes then began to water from the extreme rays of light beaming down at me from the ceiling.

'Taste will have to go,' I firmly stated.

'Taste,' they repeated. They paused for a moment. 'Mmm … interesting.' The second scientist glared at me. His mouth opned like a trap door in slow motion.

'Well, what's your reason for such an important decision. You are the boss, but we need a reason to back up your point.'

The words from the scientist's mouth just flowed into my left ear and straight out the other. I was in a dream world. I tried to calm down. I relaxed for a moment, then turned to the two scientists again.

'It's just a robot! I know that the robot clearly needs to hear, see and smell for danger and help, and needs touch to pick up things,' I attacked.

'So what's wrong with taste then?' they questioned.

I took a deep breath, then continued the conversation.

'No-one needs taste! You only use it to enjoy sweetness in food, but as for that it is useless. A robot doesn't need taste at all,' I replied convincingly.

The first scientist stepped away from me, then charged back to his chair and faced the other scientist, The first one whispered something to the other. They both turned to me, once again, with a large grin across their faces.

'We are happy to say that we agree with you. As you don't think taste is so important,' they continued, 'we will remove that sense and design the robot to its best ability and to your satisfaction. It will be ready in 31 days.'

The two scientists rose to their feet, pushed their chairs away, with a little force, and walked to the door. I turned the light off and followed behind them. In an orderly file, in silence, we strolled down the stairs to the car-park below. I got my gold key out of my pocket and let it sink into the key hole of my red Porsche. All doors clicked open from the central locking system. The other scientists walked away into the distance. ▶▶

The speed rose rapidly – 100 kph, 160 kph, 190 kph, 210 kph, 250 kph! I had five minutes to get home, and the faster I went, the better it would be.

'Only a little way to go now, not that far,' I whispered to myself. Thoughts ran through my head about my difficult decision. Questions were being thrown about in my head like a tennis match being played – was my decision the right one? – If not, would the robot change things for the worst? – Would I be blamed if things went terribly wrong?

My eyes glared through the front screen at the traffic forming ahead. The shining red brake lights of the car in front became much larger and brighter. I was still in a trance. The cars got closer by the second. Before I knew it, the cars had come to a solid halt. My foot pleaded for the brakes. After searching hard, my foot made a well-gripped contact with the brake pad. I slammed my foot down hard, but it was too … late.

I opened my eyes. For a few seconds everything was in a blurred vision. It felt like my heart was pumping in my head instead of my chest. My lips quenched of thirst. My stomach rumbled like a set of drums. My arms and legs felt sore and bruised. After a little while I could just make out that in front of me was standing the scientists and numerous doctors.

'Where am I?' I cried.

'It's alright. Don't panic. You're safe now in hospital,' one scientist replied.

Food was brought to me. I struggled to sit up. I could smell the warm scent from the beans. I reached forward for a knife and fork, and got stuck into the beans and sausage that lay before my very eyes.

'No!' I screamed. 'No taste!'

'What are you talking about?' the doctors replied nervously.

'Quick, give me something else to eat. Quick, hurry!' I panicked.

Doctors and scientists ran in all directions. Everything seemed to be in panic mode.

'Here you go,' cried one of the doctors.

I felt nervous. I stared at the food that lay before me. I slowly picked up the large donut in my sweating hands. My hand moved in slow motion towards my mouth as I wondered if my taste would return. I took a large, sugar-full bite.

'No taste!' I shouted.

Teacher's comment: This is an interesting ironic tale. The student describes the actions and feelings in effective detail. I like the parallel at the end although the actual expression of the ending could be improved a little. Your language is generally accurate. A **band 2.**

Teacher's analysis: This is generally a well-sustained story with some commendable use of detail and direct speech. The idea of dealing with the relative value of the different senses is an interesting one but could, perhaps, have been developed further. The student is in control of his writing and the expression is mainly accurate. There are, however, some uncertain expressions and some choices of vocabulary lack precision, resulting in a loss of clarity. Punctuation is accurate and spelling is good. The student uses short sentences well at the beginning of the story to create a sense of urgency; however, he tends to overuse this technique and this leads to a lack of variety in the writing. Despite its merits of accuracy and structure the limitations mentioned earlier prevent the writing from being placed in band 1.

● Examples of reading passages and tasks for Assignment 3

Here are some examples of reading material that could be used as a basis for some coursework tasks, for example Cambridge IGCSE First Language English Assignment 3, and some suggestions of tasks that could be set on them. You might like to use these tasks in preparation for this assignment and think of how you would approach them. You could also think of other suitable tasks that you would like to do. After all, this is coursework and you are in control of what you do. However, whatever approach you choose to take, don't forget that you will be assessed on your understanding of the ideas you have read about in the source passages as well as your writing ability in expressing your own thoughts.

Theme parks

Here we have three different pieces of stimulus material. There is a newsletter from an American theme park reporting on a scientific survey about safety issues; an extract from a brochure from a theme park and a newspaper report describing a ride on a roller-coaster.

Studies confirm roller-coaster and amusement park safety

The amusement industry is caught in a bizarre marketing and image dilemma. On the one hand, it wants to attract adrenaline junkies to ride the latest, greatest, biggest, meanest thrill rides at its theme parks and amusement parks. With names like 'Flight of Fear', 'Mind Eraser', and 'Lethal Weapon', parks brazenly position their marquee roller-coasters as extreme adventures that invoke terror and dread. On the other hand, the industry wants to reassure park-goers that despite the wild names – not to mention the mega-heights and speeds – thrill rides are actually quite safe and innocuous.

Bombarded by a rising tide of negative media reports, claims linking thrill rides to brain injuries, a congressional move to regulate amusement parks, and other attacks against the industry, Six Flags fired back last week by releasing the results of two scientific studies.

The bottom line: Theme parks and amusement parks in general, and roller-coasters in particular, are remarkably safe.

The American Association of Neurological Surgeons and Exponent Failure Analysis Associates, a scientific engineering research firm, conducted the independent studies, which Six Flags commissioned. A panel of experts, including doctors, engineers, NASA astronauts, and industry reps helped present and interpret the studies' findings at a Washington, D.C. press conference. Among the studies' highlights:

Amusement parks and theme parks are safer than other leisure activities

Because roller-coaster and ride accidents play into our worst fears (which, as the coasters' names attest, are part of their appeal), the media tends to sensationalize them. Like airline disasters, however, the hype doesn't square with the facts.

It is estimated that 319 million people visited parks in 2001. According to the association, the U.S. Consumer Product Safety Commission estimates that 134 park guests required hospitalization in 2001 and that fatalities related to amusement rides average two per year.

Extrapolating these numbers, riders have a 1 in 24 million chance of serious injury and a more than 1 in one-and-a-half billion chance of being fatally injured.

According to the studies, the injury rate for children's wagons, golf, and folding lawn chairs are higher than amusement rides.

The report also says that injury risk rates at amusement parks held steady from 1997 to 2001 and decreased over the last two years.

There is no research linking roller-coasters and brain injuries

Compared to the sustained forces astronauts or fighter pilots experience, the g-forces coasters exert are brief. While coaster heights and speeds have been rising, rates of acceleration and g-forces have remained relatively constant and within tolerable levels.

According to the studies, being hit with a pillow or falling on an exercise mat can cause much higher g-forces than a roller-coaster.

Arthur Levine
(http://themeparks.about.com)

SOMETHING TO SCREAM ABOUT

scariest®
in the UK

apocalypse
'the scariest ride in the UK' - Gadget Show

g force
the only looping rollercoaster where you hang from the hip

shockwave
Europes only stand up rollercoaster

stormforce 10
'the best water ride in the country'

splash canyon
get wet get dizzy

maelstrom
the only gyro swing to face you outwards

pandemonium
turn your world upside down

Fear is the key on the mother of all thrill rides

Does the new horror attraction at Orlando's Universal Studios live up to the hype? Beverley Fearis thinks it's a scream.

On Universal Studios' new star attraction, the least you can do is keep your eyes open. Blink and you'll miss out on millions of dollars' worth of special effects – and, with queues for this ride expected to reach up to an hour in peak season, you're not going to have time for a second chance.

Billed as a fusion of threshold technology, high-speed roller-coaster engineering and space-age robotics, Revenge of the Mummy, according to its makers, heralds a new era in thrill rides. With 10 years of research and development behind it, the attraction carries riders at speeds of up to 45 miles per hour. It creates a smoke screen using 2,500 gallons of liquid nitrogen a day; blasts out 18,000 watts of sound through 200 speakers; conjures up flame effects with temperatures above 1,870°C; and features authentic-looking gleaming treasure made from more than 3,000 sheets of gold foil.

Breathtaking statistics aside, the key to the success of this four-minute ride is that it

Universal Studios

taps into all your physical and psychological fears – the dark, bugs, smoke, passing through doors into the unknown, falling, sudden movements, things that make you jump – in short, all the simple surprise and suspense elements of an old-fashioned ghost train. But forget the fluorescent-painted papier-mâché skeletons at the fairground, this is horror with a big, big, Hollywood budget.

'It takes the horror genre and stretches it as far as possible,' explains Stephen Sommers, director of the Mummy films and a collaborator on the attraction. 'The concept is to play against people's primal fears by fusing motion with very sophisticated special effects.'

The Mummy might not be the best film ever made (*The Mummy Returns* is slightly better) but it lends itself perfectly to a thrill ride, with

skeletons, tombs, curses, lost souls, and, of course, mummies. One of the highlights of the ride is a 6ft 8in robotic figure of a mummy that Universal claims is the most realistic and fluid animated figure ever created. But the loudest screams come when riders plunge through a smoke screen into darkness (handy tip: this is when the dreaded photograph is taken) and when the car suddenly jerks backwards. Alongside all its other firsts, this is the first roller-coaster to employ both forward and backward motion.

Unlike older rides, where the roar of the vehicle against the tracks drowns out your screams, the tracks on this one are filled with sand to minimise noise. If, like me, your language rapidly deteriorates when under extreme pressure, remember there are children around. My advice is: keep your eyes open and your mouth shut.

As its newest ride, Revenge of the Mummy is set to be the park's biggest draw, but it's just one of many exhilarating attractions at Universal's two parks – Universal Studios and the Islands of Adventure next door.

From the *Observer*, 23 May 2004

Possible tasks

1 Write a magazine article in which you analyse why people find theme parks and their rides so popular. You should also comment on why they are not dangerous. You should base your writing closely on the material printed on pages147–50.
2 Your school has arranged a trip to a theme park. Write a letter to parents who may be worried by this, explaining why their children are more likely to enjoy the experience than not. You should base your arguments on the material on pages147–50.

Gorillas in danger

This material consists of a website campaign on behalf of a conservation group and a piece of personal writing from someone who has strong feelings about the threats faced by the world's gorilla population.

Gorilla Conservation Campaign

To donate to the Emergency Gorilla Appeal Click Here!

The Wildlife Conservation Society (WCS) is the only organization in the world working to protect all of Africa's gorilla populations, specifically the world-renowned mountain gorillas, as well as the eastern lowland gorillas, and western gorillas. WCS began studying these spectacular primates in 1959 with Dr George Schaller's seminal studies of mountain gorillas in the Virunga Volcanoes region on the borders of Rwanda, Uganda and the Democratic Republic of Congo. Schaller's work paved the way for future conservation efforts and showed that gorillas were not the raging beasts of myth, but gentle, group-oriented animals, feeding primarily on plants and fruit.

WCS's research on mountain gorillas continued in the 1970s, when researchers Amy Vedder and Bill Weber launched the Mountain Gorilla Project (MGP) in Rwanda. Vedder and Weber's work on mountain gorilla ecology and how economics and human attitudes affect conservation helped save these majestic primates from what many experts at the time considered to be certain extinction. Through a combination of education outreach and ecotourism, the MGP helped rebuild mountain gorilla numbers from a low of about 250 in the late 1970s to its present count of 360 individuals. WCS continues to fund conservation projects in Rwanda, providing a much-needed institutional presence to ensure the protection of this most endangered great ape.

►►

While not nearly as well-known as mountain gorillas, eastern lowland gorillas are also endangered. Little is known about this gorilla subspecies, due primarily to the inaccessible forests where it lives. WCS conducted the first-ever comprehensive survey of eastern lowland gorillas in 1998, finding a surprisingly robust population living primarily around Kahuzi-Biega, Maiko and Virunga National Parks in Democratic Republic of Congo. Since that time, a new war involving several African nations and numerous rebel groups has enveloped the entire region. Park guards are severely limited in their ability to patrol park borders in this region, while poaching and habitat loss have become widespread. Further, eastern DR Congo has become the centre of mining operations for coltan, a naturally occurring alloy that is used in cell phone technology. Mining camps in and around parks like Kahuzi-Biega National Park have caused an increase in bushmeat hunting, and the most recent surveys indicate that gorilla numbers may be in steep decline.

Western gorillas are probably more numerous than mountain and eastern lowland gorillas combined; however, at a meeting held in Leipzig, Germany in May, 2002, gorilla experts from several countries concluded that lack of enforcement in protected areas throughout Central Africa constitutes a significant threat to western gorillas across their range. WCS scientists currently working in western gorilla range countries – the Republic of Congo, Central African Republic, Nigeria and Gabon – are helping to create management plans for gorillas through a combination of research, education and cooperation with governmental agencies in the region.

Today, the future for gorillas remains uncertain. With central Africa's human population growing quickly, pressures on both gorilla habitat and the animals themselves will only escalate. Further, growing turmoil in the area has made it difficult for conservationists to protect one of our closest relatives. It is only through the efforts of WCS and other dedicated conservationists, that continue to work closely with local people and governments, that we can expect to save the gorilla – a living symbol of the wilds of Africa.

Conservation Addendum

WCS is a member of the Bushmeat Crisis Task Force – a coalition of conservation groups monitoring the situation in Kahuzi-Biega National Park in Democratic Republic of Congo. As a result of civil war, poor security around the park has led to widespread killing of animals – including Grauer's gorillas – by people desperate for food. In 1994–1995, WCS carried out a survey of the worldwide distribution of Grauer's gorillas and found that 86% of the population was found in Kahuzi-Biega. Today, due to the region's extreme volatility, conservationists have been able to do little on-the-ground work. Even the park guards, who were disarmed when the war started, cannot patrol large areas of Kahuzi-Biega because of safety concerns. Recently, the U.S. State Department and the Bushmeat Crisis Task Force have discussed ways to alleviate the situation, including working with the different warring factions to find peace, and addressing issues of food security into the region, which would in turn take the pressure off wildlife populations.

Wildlife Conservation Society
(www.wcs.org)

Mountain Gorillas in Peril

After 10 years of respite, a new assault was perpetrated last month against mountain gorillas and their very chances for survival.

In December of 94, my husband and I visited with a peaceful family of 25 mountain gorillas in the Virunga Mountains of Zaire [Democratic Republic of Congo]. There are no words to describe what a wonderful experience it was to observe these majestic creatures, our closest relatives, in their natural habitat. The hour and a half I spent with them was to be one of my sweetest memories. But today my memories are shattered,

spoiled with blood and rage. On August 14th, Marcel (also known as Rugabo), the beautiful silverback leader of the group, and an adult female were shot to death, while trying to prevent the kidnapping of an infant.

Marcel was probably the most famous gorilla in the area, and his group was very habituated to tourists. The circumstances of the murder are still under investigation, but here is what we know today: Apparently, a ranger of the Parc National des Virungas was hired by a private collector to capture a young male gorilla. The ranger, who knew Marcel well, thought he could get away with just snatching the baby. He obviously did not count on the gorillas' protectiveness. No amount of habituation will prevent a silverback from protecting his group, or a mother her child. Now thanks to some of our fellow men's greed and stupidity there are two more names on the list of the heroic gorillas who have sacrificed their lives at the spears and guns of poachers and collectors.

Fortunately, the baby gorilla was retrieved from a truck at the Uganda border and successfully reintroduced in his family. He was named Rafiki ('friend' in Swahili) in honour of a Nairobi-based company who runs safaris in the area. Marcel and his lady were buried behind the warden's hut in Djomba, in the presence of several Zairian dignitaries. Their deaths are not only a tragedy for their group (if there isn't a male capable of taking over the role of silverback, the group may disintegrate and wander aimlessly in the forest at the mercy of poachers), they put a serious dent in the whole species' chances for survival.

There are only about 650 mountain gorillas left in the world, half of which live in the Parc National des Virungas in Zaire, and the other half in neighbouring Rwanda and Uganda. Each time one dies, it reduces the genetic pool available for their reproduction. Before this year, there had been no gorillas killed since the murder of Dian Fossey, the famous gorilla conservationist, in 1985. Unfortunately, Marcel and his female are not the only mountain gorillas who died this year. Four were shot in Uganda in March; a silverback, named Salama, died from unknown causes in Zaire; and just a couple of weeks ago, another silverback, named Luwaya, was found shot in the Virungas. Luwaya's death brings the count to eight, a terrible loss in a population of 650.

Most of the deaths are attributable to poachers who kill the gorillas for their meat or to capture infants. The problem has become acute in the past year due to the presence of more than 750,000 Rwandan refugees in the camps of Goma near the Parc des Virungas. On August 22nd, the Zairian soldiers tried to force some refugees, most of them Hutu gunmen responsible for killing about 500,000 Tutsis, back to Rwanda, but mostly succeeded in sending 60,000 of them into the mountains to escape the expulsions. The presence of the refugees increases the pressure on the endangered mountain gorillas. According to a study conducted for the UN, 18 square kilometres of forest have already been destroyed by refugees cutting wood for fuel, and 78 square kilometres are badly damaged. Deforestation and the invasion of refugees in the National Park puts the gorillas at risk, not only from poaching, but also from being pushed higher up the mountains, where they may suffer respiratory problems.

One of the most present problems, however, comes from the drop in tourism that all this turmoil has caused. The National Parks get most of their revenues from the tourists who come to see the gorillas. In Djomba, a visit costs $120 per person and up to 8 tourists go each day. If there are no tourists, close to a $1000 a day and $365,000 a year is lost to the Park authorities and, therefore, taken away from the gorillas' protection. If the Park is not protected, there will be no limits to the damage made to the mountain gorillas' only habitat on earth, which would undoubtedly lead to their extinction.

You probably can't solve the refugee problem in Zaire, but there are ways you can help. Visiting the mountain gorillas is the best way to relieve their plight. Not only will you help guarantee their continued protection, you will see for yourself what wonderful and gentle creatures mountain gorillas are. Although going to Rwanda is not recommended, you can still visit the gorillas in Uganda or Zaire. As Chris McDonald from Rafiki Africa puts it: 'We have experienced no increased levels of risk at Djomba and the locals remain as friendly as ever. The fact is that the gorilla sanctuary is approached from the Uganda side of the Virunga mountains and the problems facing Zaire, as far as the 1,000,000 refugees from Rwanda are concerned, may as well be thousands of miles away.' If you would like to go, please contact Kilimanjaro Adventure Travel on the web at www.kilimanjaro.com.

You can also help by sending donations to various animal protection groups. The World Society for the Protection of Animals is running the EscApe campaign, specifically dedicated to the survival of the great apes. We are also hoping to start a 'Marcel Fund' in connection with the Dian Fossey Gorilla Fund (UK), in order to build a visitor education centre that will help the public understand the gorillas, their habitat, and future survival. Please check back with us to see what the status is and how you can help.

Stephanie Hancock,
www.kilimanjaro.com

Possible tasks

1 Using the reading material on pages 151–54, write the words of a pamphlet aimed at younger children, explaining the dangers faced by gorillas and what could be done to help protect them.
2 Using the details contained in the reading material on pages 151–54, write the script of a radio discussion programme titled 'What Makes Animals So Important Anyway?' featuring Stephanie Hancock, a representative from the Wildlife Conservation Society and yourself as Chair, who, for the sake of argument, adopts a position opposed to conservation issues.

Coursework checklist

When your coursework is assessed, the following points will all be taken into consideration. If you also take them into consideration when you check and revise your work before submitting your portfolio, you could gain yourself a better grade!

1 Is the content:
   - interesting
   - entertaining
   - enjoyable?
2 Does it achieve the assessment objectives for continuous writing, proving that you can:
   - articulate experience and express what is thought, felt and imagined
   - sequence facts, ideas and opinions
   - use a range of appropriate vocabulary
   - use register appropriate to audience and context
   - make accurate use of spelling, punctuation and grammar?
3 Is it well structured? Is it easy to follow and does it move sensibly from beginning to end?
4 Is the style appropriate for the purpose of the piece?
5 How accurate is the writing? How good is the:
   - spelling
   - grammar
   - punctuation?

Speaking and listening skills

What is tested and how?

Assessment in oral work (i.e. speaking and listening skills) does not contribute directly to your grade in Cambridge IGCSE First Language English. Candidates doing Syllabus 0522 are required to undertake this aspect of the IGCSE syllabus and the grade they achieve will be recorded separately on their certificate. In other syllabuses, it is an optional element, in which case your teacher might have decided to enter your class for the written examination only. However, whether they are assessed or not, speaking and listening are bound to be an integral part of your English lessons, and being able to speak in English and understand what is said to you in reply are hugely important skills. It's also worth remembering that if you write a script for your written papers, you will produce a better piece if you have thought about how to speak interestingly and communicate clearly.

In Chapters 4 and 5 we looked at the skills involved in writing for different purposes and for different audiences. Similar skills are needed for speaking. If you are a high court judge about to sentence someone to ten years in jail, you are going to speak rather differently from someone who is talking to a group of friends about whether to go to the cinema or to go shopping. Even in school, you adapt your speaking style to different situations – perhaps without really thinking about it: you are bound to find yourself in a mix of formal and informal situations, talking with adults and with your peers, talking about school work and your leisure time, and so on.

The following pages relate specifically to the Cambridge IGCSE First Language English Syllabus, but much of the advice and the suggested tasks are appropriate for any examination syllabus that tests speaking and listening skills. In Cambridge IGCSE First Language English there are two methods of assessment of speaking and listening:

- the test
- coursework.

You probably already know that for the written part of your English Language examination you will receive a letter grade, A, B, C and so on. For the speaking and listening test, you will also receive a letter grade from A to G.

The test is conducted by an examiner who is usually your teacher, although some schools do bring in specialists to do it. The test lasts about ten minutes, broken down into:

- 3–4 minutes for the **individual task**
- 6–7 minutes for a **discussion arising from the individual task**.

Both aspects of the test are explained in more detail below.

How is the test marked?

The individual task and discussion are recorded and the recording is sent to a moderator who is appointed by the examination board. The moderator receives a number of recordings and compares them with the standards that have been set. He/She will decide whether you have been assessed at the right standard. If he/she agrees with your teacher's marks, the results will simply be sent to the examining board; if the moderator doesn't quite agree with your teacher then he/she might adjust your marks slightly.

Study tip

To build your confidence in speaking, record some practice pieces. You could start by reading something out loud, just to get used to the sound of your own voice on the recording. Once you have done this, make your practice as close to the situation you will face in the test as possible – in other words, find a willing partner, do some preparation and then have a go! If you manage to do this a few times then you will feel much more confident when it comes to the test itself.

The individual task

Before you take the test, think of a topic that interests you. You should be able to talk to your teacher on this topic for between three and four minutes, without interruption or prompting. Your talk can be formal or informal; you can deliver it as a presentation or as a speech.

Your talk should show evidence of your ability to:

- articulate experience and express what is thought, felt and imagined
- present facts, ideas and opinions in a sustained, cohesive order
- communicate clearly, fluently and purposefully as an individual and in dialogue with other speakers
- use register appropriate to audience and context.

It is important that you show interest in and enthusiasm for the subject about which you choose to talk. You are allowed to use cue cards to prompt you about the key points but you should not read from a prepared script; this is, after all, a test of your **speaking** not reading ability. You may also, if you wish, use a limited range of visual aids to support your talk but remember that you have only a limited time and too many such aids can inhibit what you have to say.

The discussion

The discussion will take the form of a conversation with the teacher/examiner about issues arising from your talk on your chosen topic. The teacher/examiner will not take an aggressive stance but will encourage you to expand positively on what you have said. In order to make the best impression, it is important that you have prepared your topic thoroughly. Some of the questions you are asked may well require you to refer to factual information additional to that included in your talk and also to develop or defend your point of view. The teacher/examiner will have taken notes while you were talking, so it is important that you pay careful attention to the questions that you are asked: your **listening** skills are being tested as well as your speaking ones!

The conversation should last about six or seven minutes and the comments made by the teacher/examiner will be kept to the minimum to allow you to express yourself as fully and as fluently as you can.

Choosing a topic

It is up to you to choose a topic that you want to introduce and discuss in the test. The only restriction on the choice is that your teacher/examiner must be happy to discuss the topic with you. Make sure you choose a topic that you know something about and are able to discuss. This may sound obvious but students have been known to choose topics which sounded impressive, but about which they knew very little, if anything! You might consider these possibilities.

Do you have a hobby?

You might collect stamps; you might go ballroom dancing every week; you might breed fish; you might have a pet boa constrictor which has to be fed on small live rodents; you might knit socks. The point about a hobby is that presumably it is something you enjoy and find interesting. You should be able to interest other people in it. By way of preparation, ask yourself the following questions.

● Why did I start this hobby?
● When did I start?
● How much time do I spend on my hobby?
● Why do I enjoy it?
● Is there anything I can take with me to help me introduce the topic?
● How else might I make my hobby interesting for the teacher/examiner?

Then you can plan your introduction. You might do it in such a way that there are some obvious questions for the teacher/examiner to ask in the discussion.

Do you travel much?

Many of you might be lucky enough to have travelled widely; you may have been to places that you have loved; you may have been to places that you have hated. Either way, you should be able to talk about them in an interesting way. Again, you need to prepare, and the following points might help.

● Make a list of all the places that you have visited.
● Group similar places together.
● Pick out the places that you most liked.
● Pick out those places that you didn't like at all.
● Consider what was most important to you when thinking about a place – the people, the buildings, the scenery?
● If you were to pick your favourite place, which would it be?

What do you want to do as a career?

You may have a very clear idea about what you want to do as a future career, or you may have a part-time job that will provide you with material for your discussion. Do you baby-sit, work in a local shop, run your own website service? Some of you might be hoping that your part-time job will expand into a future career; for others it may just be a means of earning enough money to be able to go out with friends at the weekend.

Some of you might have been sent on work experience by your school. Again, through work experience you might have discovered your future career path. Alternatively, you might have been very bored or you might have hated every moment of your experience. Even so, you will have learned something for the future.

However you have gained your experience, whatever your ideas, this might be a topic which would work for you. Ask yourself the following questions.

● Do I know what I want to do as a career?
● How did I get this idea?
● Was I influenced by others rather than making up my own mind? (For instance, do you want to do the same job as one of your parents?)
● Why am I sure I will enjoy this job?
● How important is the salary to me?
● Do I think it will be a job for life?

Are you passionate about a particular issue?

'I am a vegetarian! No one should eat meat. It is unnecessary and barbaric.'

'Animals should not be used to test products for us humans. The plight of animals that are used to test cosmetics is disgraceful. Even testing medicines on animals should not happen; use human volunteers.'

'All rubbish should be recycled. We are destroying our own planet with our pollution. People who abuse our planet should be fined huge amounts. We have to think of our children and grandchildren.'

'They are my favourite pop group. I would go to the ends of the earth to see them. Their last record was the most exciting thing I have ever heard. I know some people disagree with me but they simply don't have any soul.'

'School uniform should go!'

If you choose to talk about an issue that you feel passionate about, you must be able to talk without being overdramatic and you must have clear reasons to use to convince your listener. If you start off by advocating that all school uniforms should be burnt and the teacher/examiner argues against you, you will not do very well if all you can do is keep repeating 'I hate it!'. So decide:

- What is my subject?
- Why do I feel strongly about it?
- What do I need to say to make sure the listener understands the subject?
- What are likely to be the arguments on the other side and how will I answer them?

Is your family interesting?

It is perfectly possible that your aunt is an astronaut. Your father might have been an Olympic athlete. Your grandmother was possibly the first woman to sail around the world single-handed. Your brother might be the world pie-eating champion. In other words, there might be members of your family who have achieved outstanding success. If so, there is little doubt that you could talk about them in a fascinating way. You might even be able to bring in a lump of moon rock or an Olympic gold medal to help in your introduction!

However, you might believe your family to be interesting for far more simple reasons. Perhaps you have lived in a variety of countries and have had to adapt to frequent moves. Perhaps you come from a very large family who are involved in a wide range of activities, which means that your family life is a non-stop whirlwind.

If this is the topic for you, then you must decide on your way into it.

- Who or what am I going to talk about?
- Would others find the person I am going to talk about interesting?
- Are there things which I should keep private?
- If the teacher/examiner asks me a question I don't want to answer, how am I going to get out of it? (There is no problem with politely declining to answer a question and moving on.)
- Are there any small items I could take to the test that will be useful to illustrate my points?

Have you been fascinated by a book you have read, or a play or film you have seen?

If you were to choose this topic, you would find it quite straightforward because the first thing you would have to do is make sure that the teacher/examiner understood what you were talking about. You would have to reiterate the plot of a novel, however briefly; you would have to tell the story of a film or a play and say who was in it, and perhaps why their performances were so good.

You may well find that you have to take the lead more than with some of the other topics. One point remains central, though: you must not only be able to tell the teacher/examiner what the book, film or play was about, but you must also be able to explain, perhaps in some detail, why it was so special for you.

Does a particular person interest you?

A wide-open topic if ever there was one, and many of the points and ideas discussed in this section lead you in. Your person might be a member of your family, it might be a singer or an actor. It might be someone from history who fascinates you.

- Choose your person.
- Make sure you know about your subject in detail and can interest a listener.

Study tip

Remember that the discussion will develop from your individual talk. The teacher/examiner will have been listening very carefully to what you have said and will have some questions to ask. He/She may also have some ideas of his/her own and will want to see what you think of them. In order to respond well, you need to:

- listen very carefully
- take your time in answering thoughtfully.

● Coursework

If your school has decided to assess your speaking and listening skills by coursework, you will be assessed by your teacher three times during the course in three different speaking and listening tasks. These will involve:

- **Task 1 – an individual activity** (like that required by the test as described on page 157) in which you talk about a topic that is interesting or important to you.
- **Task 2 – a pair-based activity** in which you and a partner (either a classmate or the teacher) take part in a role play or an interview about a topic of interest, for example an argument between neighbours or a mock interview for a position of importance within the community.
- **Task 3 – a group activity** in which you are part of a small group of students who are involved in a discussion relating to a particular scenario, for example, a panel of experts discussing the performance of a local sports team in an important game, etc.

The suggestions given about discussion topics on the previous pages could equally form the basis of the individual activity for those of you whose speaking and listening skills are assessed by coursework.

What is certain is that your teacher will want to give you the opportunity to speak and listen in a variety of contexts. It is worth thinking about the different purposes for which we need to talk. We might need to:

- explain
- describe
- narrate, read or recite
- analyse in detail
- imagine something and interest the listener in it
- put some ideas together and then explore them, either with a partner or in a group
- discuss
- argue (not in the sense of having a row but of putting forward your view)
- persuade.

Remember that it is always your job to decide why you are talking and therefore how you should speak.

Remember also that with coursework there is no need to be nervous, because if things go wrong you and your teacher can always decide that you can have another go later. But then, things won't go wrong!

Index

Acknowledgements

The publishers would like to thank the following for permission to reproduce copyright material:

Text credits

pp.07–08: Arthur C. Clarke, *Voice Across the Sea* (Frederick Muller/Harper & Row, 1958), reproduced by permission of David Higham; **pp.08–09:** Ian Burrell, 'Thank God…it's a miracle', the *Independent* (1998), *www.independent.co.uk*, reproduced by permission of ESI Media; **pp.11–13:** Philip Smith, 'The lost lagoon', adapted, *http://www.guardian.co.uk/travel/2008/nov/argentina-esteros-del-ibera* (29 November, 2008) copyright Guardian News & Media Ltd 2008, reproduced by permission of Guardian News & Media Ltd; **pp.16–18:** Jill Ker Conway, *The Road from Coorain: An Australian Memoir*, published by William Heinemann, reproduced by permission of The Random House Group Limited; **pp.19–20:** R.K. Narayan, 'Lawley Road', *Malgudi Days* (William Heinemann, 1992), reproduced by permission of The Random House Group Limited; **pp.21–22:** Esther Hautzig, The Endless Steppe (Puffin Books, 1993), copyright © 1969 by Esther Hautzig, reproduced by permission of Penguin Books Ltd and A.M. Heath Co. Ltd; **pp.23–24:** H.G. Wells, The First Men in the Moon (George Newnes, 1901), reprinted by permission of United Agents on behalf of The Literary Executors of the Estate of H.G. Wells; **pp.26–27:** Paul Harris, 'Hell and high water', adapted, the *Observer* (27 August, 2006) copyright Guardian News & Media Ltd 2006, reproduced by permission of Guardian News & Media Ltd; **pp.29–30:** Michael Palin, *Pole to Pole* (BBC Books, 1995); **p.35:** Michael Palin, *New Europe* (Weidenfeld & Nicolson, 2007), reproduced by permission of Orion Publishing Group; **pp.37–38:** 'Nightmare Neighbours', adapted, *Which? Magazine*; **p.39:** 'Pompeii exhibition opens at the National Museum of Singapore' *http://archaeologynewsnetwork.blogspot.co.uk/2010/10/pompeii-exhibition-opens-at-national.html#.UWV10OXiNF10* (18 October, 2010); **pp.40–41:** Jennifer Rosenberg, 'The Channel Tunnel', adapted, *http://history1900s.about.com/od/1990s/qt/Channel-Tunnel-Opens.htm*; **pp.42–43:** Tracy McVeigh, 'Britain's women footballers use social media to promote game ignored by press', the *Observer* (8 April, 2012) copyright Guardian News & Media, reproduced by permission of Guardian News & Media Ltd; **pp.43–44:** Gretchen Reynolds, 'Dieting vs. Exercise for Weight Loss', *http:well.blogs.nytimes.com/2012/08/01/dieting-vs-exercise-for-weight-loss/*; **pp.47–48:** 'Genetically Modified Foods', Young People's Trust for the Environment (YPTE), *http://www.ypte.org.uk/environmental/genetically-modified-foods/6*; **p.49:** John Taylor Gatto, 'Why Schools Don't Educate', *http://www.naturalchild.org/guest/john_gatto.html* (January 31, 1990); **pp.51–52:** Karina Wilson, 'Early Advertising', *http://www.mediaknowall.com/as_alevel/Advertising/advertising.php?pageID=history*, reproduced by permission of the author; **pp.52–53:** 'Visit to Efteling Theme Park', adapted, *http://www.indianmomsconnect.com/2013/01/02visit-it-to-efteling-theme-park/* (2 January, 2013), reproduced by permission of Vibha (Chatty Wren); **p.54:** Sheryl Garratt, 'Cheesy…but charming', adapted, the *Observer* (25 November, 2001) copyright Guardian News & Media Ltd 2001, reproduced by permission of Guardian News & Media Ltd; **p.56:** UniChem Pharmacies, Inc., 'Sports injuries'; **pp.57–59:** Suzanne Moore, 'We're told that school uniforms are about preparing our kids for the 'real world': Do we want a world full of dull conformists?', adapted, the *Guardian* (29 August, 2012) copyright Guardian News & Media Ltd 2012, reproduced by permission of Guardian News & Media Ltd;

pp.60–63: Doris Lessing, 'Flight', *The Habit of Loving* (Grafton, 1973; Flamingo, 1993); **pp.71–72:** David Jones, 'Among all the uplifting biographies in these Games, Kylie's is particularly inspirational', *Daily Mail* (5 September, 2012), reproduced by permission of Solo Syndication; **pp.76–77:** Jane E. Brody, 'Protecting children from pool accidents', the *New Straits Times* (5 July, 1994), reproduced by permission of the New Straits Times Press (M) Bhd;

p.81: Brian Ward, 'Noise' *The Environment and Health* (Frankin Watts, 1989) and Department of the Environment, Transport and the Regions (DETR);

pp.83–84: C. Navaratnam, 'Dangerous balancing act to get to and return from school', the *New Straits Times* (8 July, 1994), reproduced by permission of the New Straits Times Press (M) Bhd; **pp.84–85:** Victor Hugo, *Les Miserables* (1862), translated by Norman Denny (Folio Press, 1976), © 1976, The Folio Society, reproduced by permission of The Folio Society; **pp.90–92:** 'Why adopt a dolphin?', Whale & Dolphin Copnservation (WDC) UK, *http://www.adoptadolphin.tv* (2012);

pp.96–97: Robert Ballard, *The Discovery of the Titanic* (Orion, 1995);

pp.98–99: 'Threatened Species', The Worldwatch Institute, *www.worldwatch.org* (2000) and International Union for Conservation (IUCN) homepage screenshot, *www.redlist.org* (2013); **pp.100–101:** Sam Selvon, *A Drink of Water* (Nelson Thornes, 1968); **pp.103–105:** Khamsing Srinawk, 'The Gold-Legged Frog', *The Politician and Other Stories* (Oxford University Press, 1992); **pp.105–106:** Facts and figures about the Arctic and climate change, WWF-Canada Global Arctic Programme, *www.panda.org.arctic* (2012), reproduced by permission of WWF-Canada; **p.123:** A.S. Neill, *Summerhill* (Pelican, 1970), reproduced by permission of Summerhill School; **pp.125–126:** Guy de Maupassant, 'An Uncomfortable Bed', *The Lock and Key Library, Vol.5: Modern French Stories*, edited by Julian Hawthorne (New York: The Review of Reviews Co., 1909); **pp.147–148:** Arthur Levine, 'White Knuckles Are the Worst of It', *http://themeparks.about.com* (2003); **p.150:** Beverley Fearis, 'Fear is the key on the mother of all thrill rides', the *Observer* (23 May, 2004) copyright Guardian News & Media Ltd 2004, reproduced by permission of Guardian News & Media; **pp.151–152:** 'Gorilla Conservation Campaign', *www.wcs.org*, reproduced by permission of Wildlife Conservation Society; **pp.153–154:** Stephanie Hancock, 'Mountain Gorillas in Peril', *www.kilimanjaro.com*.

CD text credits

In alphabetical order: Gerald Durrell: extract from *My Family and Other Animals* (Penguin Books, 1959); Arthur Grimble: 'Catching Octopus', extract adapted from *A Pattern of Islands* (John Murray, 1952); Andrew Martin: 'The Glacier Express', adapted from the *Guardian* (16 March, 2004), copyright Guardian News & Media Ltd 2004, reproduced by permission of Guardian News & Media Ltd; Maternity & Infant: 'Safe as Houses' and 'Child-proofing your home', adapted from www.maternityandinfant.i.e./toddler-child-/safe-houses; Anna McGrory: 'Gripping stuff', adapted from the *Guardian* 22 July, 2000), copyright Guardian News & Media Ltd, reproduced by permission of Guardian News & Media Ltd; Michael Palin: extract from 'Tiger Leaping Gorge', adapted from *Himalaya* (Phoenix, 2009), and extract from 'Oriental Star Number 1', adapted from *Full Circle* (Phoenix, 2009), both reproduced by permission of Orion Publishing Group; Nick Pope: extract adapted from The Cosford Incident from *www.nickpope.net/cosford-incident.htm*, reproduced by permission of Nick Pope; Ben Ross: Tiger's

Nest Monastery', adapted from the *Independent* (17 December, 2011), *www.independent.co.uk* reproduced by permission of ESI Media.

Every effort has been made to contact rights holders, acknowledge ownership of copyright and secure permission. The publishers will be glad to make good any omissions or correct any errors brought to their notice at the earliest opportunity.

Photo credits

p.1 *t* © Friedrich Stark/Alamy; **p.1** *b* © Getty Images/Fuse; **p.2** © Getty Images/ iStockphoto; **p.5** © Getty Images/Jupiterimages; **p.12** ©Vesalio – Fotolia; **p.16** © J. Hartley/Panos; **p.39** © Robert Harding Picture Library Ltd/Alamy; **p.41** © Herbert Ortner/http://commons.wikimedia.org/wiki/File:Eurostar_3012_ Waterloo.jpg/http://creativecommons.org/licenses/by/3.0/deed.en; **p.53** © Efteling bv; **p.58** © paylessimages – Fotolia; **p.71** © Mark Davidson/Alamy; **p.76** © Patrik Giardino/CORBIS; **p.84** © Michael le Poer Trench/ArenaPAL; **p.91** © WDC/Charlie Phillips; **p.92** © WDC/Charlie Phillips; **p.96** © Ralph White/ Corbis; **p.149** © Drayton Manor; **p.150** © Ian Dagnall/Alamy; **p.151** © Joe McDonald/Corbis; **p.153** © Image Source/Corbis

t = top, *c* = centre, *b* = bottom, *l* = left, *r* = right

Every effort has been made to trace all copyright holders, but if any have been inadvertently overlooked the publishers will be pleased to make the necessary arrangements at the first opportunity.